INSIDE

It was, I would roam around that place all the time and I always dreamed about going to Paris so, a lot of these things fit in. But the conception we would have had what was going on was, well you know it develops. Everything is put into question again and there was the Bauhaus, late 20's and 30's and there was the Russians, there was a whole lot of things that we vaguely knew about and we all, when I say we, there was a bunch of kids late 40's, beginning of the 50's in Paris who decided they wanted to be artists, you know, and artists at that time meant being a painter. Was true that it was just a moment when being an artist was also beginning to be conceived as being a whole lot of different things, and there were examples like that of people who'd come out of Bauhaus, you know, there were Moholy-Nagi, there was Max Bill and there were people who.... even Leger was somebody who wasn't associated with Bauhaus but I think he was a man who did painting, theatre sets, he did films, he did applied arts, he did a lot of different things but, in Paris, that wasn't yet really something that existed. It exists nowadays really in Paris, I mean, an artist can conceivably be doing a commercial advertising film, he can do stuff for clothes and so on, but people who did that in Paris at that time were, I mean in the history of modern art in Paris, were not really well considered. I mean there's an example like Sonia Delauny and her husband and they were, they were put down because it was considered that they were selling out doing commercial work and so on. I think the, it's the....

DP That's amazing, that's very surprising...

INSIDE PHOTOGRAPHY

INTERVIEWS WITH TEN EDITORS

David Brittain
and Clinton Cahill

Dewi Lewis Publishing

Published in 2013 by
Dewi Lewis Publishing
8 Broomfield Road
Heaton Moor
Stockport SK4 4ND
England
www.dewilewispublishing.com

ISBN 978-1-907893-46-9

Three of these interviews, Jack Schofield, Bill Jay and Carl Chiarenza, appeared in 8 magazine and its blog in abridged versions.

Cover photograph: David Brittain
Layout and cover design: Clinton Cahill

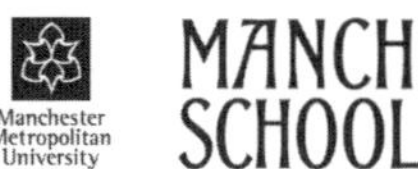

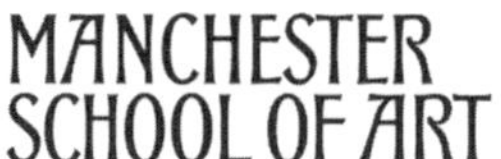

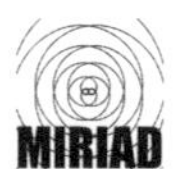

Acknowledgements

The use of first-person testimony as history can be contentious. This is because it is based on memory which is often, if not unreliable, then subject to revision over time, opening the way for distortions. Nevertheless, this method has been used to great effect in some celebrated photographic publications, notably "Dialogue with Photography" (Cooper and Hill). One of the most enthusiastic advocates of oral history is the novelist Haruki Murakami. In his book which concerns the 1995 sarin attack on the Tokyo transport system, he writes, "The truth of 'whatever is told' will differ, however slightly from what actually happened... This, however, does not make it a lie; it is unmistakably the truth, albeit in another form." It is not so much 'truth' that interests me however, but the 'perspective', and that can often attain clarity with the passing of time.

These interviews began with an initial exchange, either face-to-face or through email or in one case in letters. Each interview was edited, then where possible, texts were sent back to the interviewee soliciting comments and additions. New, amended versions of the transcripts evolved out of this process that, while retaining the "Q and A" format, became something else. My collaborator/co-author Clinton Cahill began discussing what this might be. To this end, we deployed text and design to explore the borders, if you like, between the "I" that interviews and the "I" that "writes" through the words of others, the interviewees. We decided to include an earlier draft of my interview with Richard West, hoping the disparities between the original exchange and the final version would shed light on the interview process.

My gratitude to Bill Johnson and Sally Petty who generously offered advice and enabled access to the research library at the Visual Studies Workshop, comprising over 1400 periodicals; also to Rachel Stuhlman at George Eastman House. Thank you to John Hyatt and Philip Sykas at Manchester Metropolitan University, and special thanks to all interviewees who made their time available then agreed to make checks and revisions. I am also grateful to Max Houghton for her valuable editorial advice.

Finally, I want to thank Clinton Cahill whose design concept comprises a parallel text to this publication. Clinton is interested in both the negotiated nature of the interview process and the range of technologies that were deployed. During the period between the first and last interviews (2002 to 2010), my recording and storage techniques changed from analogue to digital. With the exception of the late Bill Jay, who insisted on sending his responses by conventional mail, most interviews were made face-to-face. For convenience two were conducted via email.

s were sketches for a movie – he sai
ip for a movie – is that right?

Well, maybe I said that to him but I guess, you know, it's all part of one thing, I really don't.... I Mean they're very different as far as, very different making a movie and making a photograph.

Which do you prefer, or is that a stupid question?

Well, it's not a stupid question but It's a hard question to answer and it doesn't..... what I like about photography..... I have this nostalgia, mean everybody has a nostalgia for when they were kids, you know, olescents, so everything's possible; and there's something you also have ostalgia........

When you exhibited, did New York feature?

ey weren't exhibited, it was just a ho
 no real framework f
 Famil

Contents

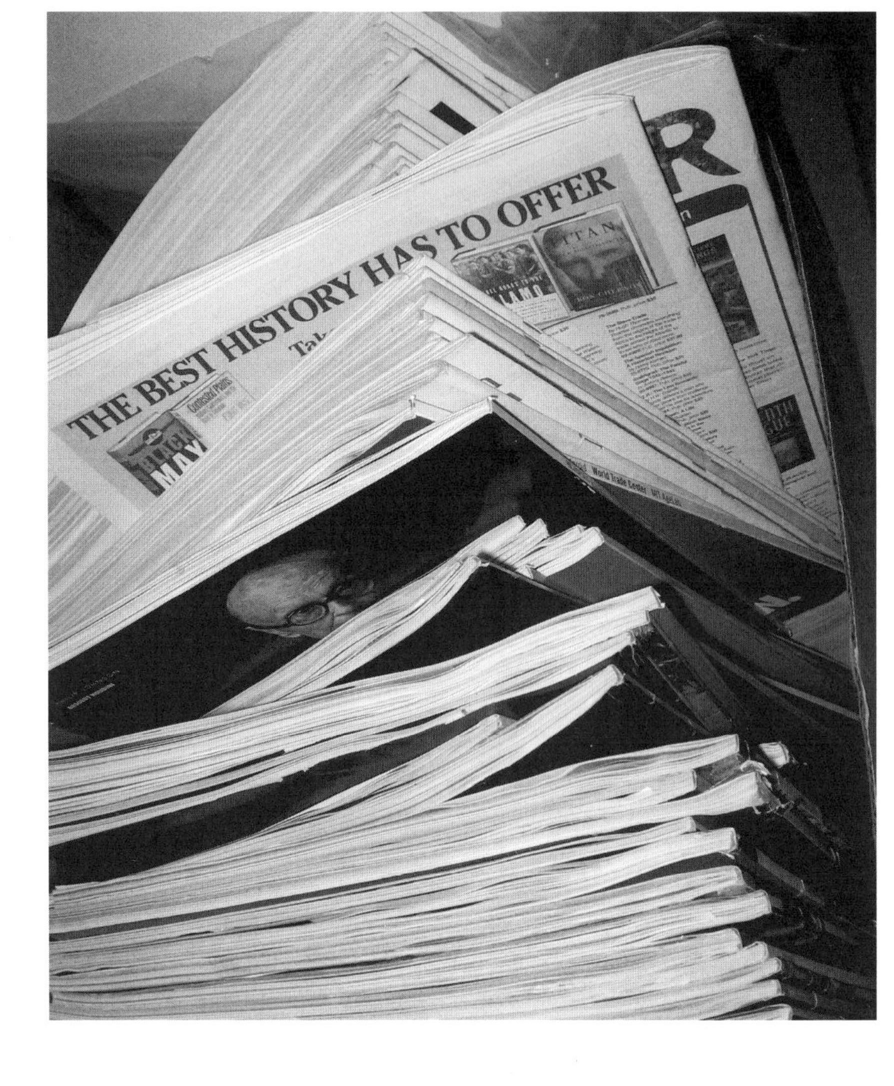
THE BEST HISTORY HAS TO OFFER

The Photographers' Magazine: *Towards A Type*

Specialist photography magazines have existed almost since the announcement of the invention of photography in 1839 and many are still in existence today – in both conventional and electronic formats. In their book 'The History of Photography', Helmut and Alison Gernsheim list 29 photographic journals that began publication prior to 1862, including the first in English (founded in New York, 1850). Some of these spoke to and on behalf of the leisured, educated amateur. Increasingly, as the photographic process became industrialised, new titles reflected the interests of professionals. Towards the end of the nineteenth century, in parallel with the advent of large-circulation magazines for snap shooters, titles emerged to promote the practice, critical appraisal and appreciation of photography as an art. This type of publication is the one that concerns us here, the embodiment of a complex mixture of altruism and self-interest. By far the most famous is 'Camera Work', founded by Alfred Stieglitz in 1903 at the dawn of the age of half-tone reproduction and coinciding with the rise of the modernist avant-garde. Over the years 'Camera Work' with its critical and polemical articles and high production values, has come to epitomise the magazine of art photography, for better or worse. As the focus of postmodern critical attention, Stieglitz's luxury title highlighted the key role of this kind of publication within its field. Since 'Camera Work', many such titles have fulfilled similar functions for their various informed readers within the broader photographic culture in which they exist and co-exist. These would include linking photographers with their peers, disseminating information in the form of opinion, reviews and news, validating photographic styles, tastes and reputations, and advocacy.

The focus of this book is the practices and attitudes of the editors of ten, maybe eleven, twentieth-century art photography magazines. It is not my intention to engage in a critical analysis of each of these publications as "texts", or to ignore their "materiality" (the design consciously references this) but rather to propose that they represent a special type of magazine, despite differences. As manifestations of the aspirations, fantasies and prejudices of readers, such magazines are part of the sociology of photography. And yet relatively little is known about them, the variations within the type and the identities and activities of editors and the influence they may exert.

Data suggests[1] that the 1970s was a boom time for photography magazines and it coincided with attempts to map the bohemian quarter of the sector. In 1977 the

[1] I draw my conclusion from a search of the periodicals collection of SUNY at Brockport. Data reveals a gradual increase in the number of photography magazines subscribed to. The first titles appear in 1970 and there is a peak in 1980 that tails off five years later. It must be stressed that figures do not reveal the names of titles.

unsung Bill Johnson at the magazine 'Afterimage', identified a "core" of around 40 cultural titles[2]. Bill's list is useful, if somewhat confounding, because in addition to well-established art photography titles (for instance 'Aperture') there are fine art magazines, such as 'Artscanada', 'Art in America' and 'Studio International' and even a mainstream magazine, the 'New York Sunday Times'. The year following the 'Afterimage' survey, the Swiss title 'Print Letter' identified 42 titles internationally that conformed to the criterion: "magazines that deal with photography as art"[3]. Inevitably there was some overlapping between the lists, suggesting perhaps the formation of a vague kind of consensus. One obvious flaw with such surveys was the lack of a working consensus as to what constitutes "art photography". I suggest that this term is contingent and mutable. For a period of 10 years (1991-2001) I edited an "art photography" magazine based in London called 'Creative Camera' [4] that featured in both surveys. Part of my task was to become acquainted with affiliated titles from around the world that, by this time, comprised an informal network (at different times it included 'Hyperphoto' and 'Catalog' from Scandinavia, 'Perspektief' from the Netherlands, 'Luna Cornea' from Mexico, 'Photographies' from France, 'PhotoVision' from Spain, 'European Photography' from Germany, 'Camera Austria' from Austria, 'Photofile' from Australia and from the US, 'Aperture'). I became convinced that such titles, while very individual in their defence and advocacy of an art of photography, displayed many significant common traits. My search for these traits began in the archives of the Visual Studies Workshop and the George Eastman House, both in Rochester. The first task was to find out how many "art" titles existed during a given period. Knowing that many editors took titles from the technology and practice of photography, I started with keywords such as camera, image, lens, light, photo, photographer and so on, confining my search to the 1960s, seventies and eighties – in other words a decade prior to and following the peak years for this kind of title. From a long list I eliminated anything that fell outside my area of interest (for instance, purely technical magazines and, regretfully, foreign language titles)[5]. But this still left a baffling array of types of publication – each with its core reader (from view camera and stereo enthusiasts to historians), particular format and production values (from a mimeographed foolscap page to a perfect bound codex), frequency (monthly to annually), text to image ratio (from mostly textual or mostly image-based) and distinct attitude. At the end of this long process I had a manageable short list and even a tentative category for this kind of title: the photographer's magazine. I knew the term "portfolio magazine" but rejected it as meaningless. I decided the term "art photography" magazine was unhelpful. In any case "photography" always implies a narrow set of practices. My favoured term reflects a conviction[6] that it's photographers that establish such titles. The catalyst tends to be

[2] Johnson W.,(1977) 'An Index to Articles on Photography' *Afterimage* November.

[3] Misani M.(1978) 'Survey of Photography Magazines', *Print Letter* 13.

[4] In 2000 'Creative Camera' became co-opted into a short-lived new title, DPICT[5] While many exciting titles were foreign, it would have been a challenge to translate both languages and cultural contexts.

frustration with the low esteem with which photography is treated, with lack of access to exhibition facilities, lack of intelligent discourse on photography and so on. So it is practitioners with grievances and strong agendas that tend to shape the attitude of the titles that other practitioners read, support and identify with..

The photographer's magazine differs significantly from the fine arts magazine such as 'Art in America' that occasionally covers photography and also from a title such as 'Vanity Fair' or 'National Geographic' that stylishly showcases great images[7]. In the former, discussions around photography take place within a larger context; photographers' magazines, by contrast, put photography at the centre of their thinking to keep specialist readers up to speed with trends. Editors will usually be specialists too, rather than the professional journalists trusted by big publishing houses, and will be known to readers for their practice within photography. The roster of photographer-editors includes of course Stieglitz, Minor White, Carl Chiarenza, Nathan Lyons (all US), Joan Fontcuberta (Spain), Pablo Ortiz Monasterio (Mexico) and Andreas Müller-Pohle (Germany) and in Britain John Duncan co-editor of 'Source'. Others come from journalism (Derek Bishton, Bill Jay and Colin Jacobson) or from theory and curating (Geoffrey Batchen) and are generally supported in their work by photographers. Precedents for this include Edward Steichen who was in partnership with Tom Maloney at 'US Camera' and Tony Ray-Jones and David Hurn that were mentors to Bill Jay at 'Creative Camera'. All this is to say that these particular magazines address the subject from inside something called the "photographic community", commanding strong loyalties among discriminating readers.

Compared even with the average fine art title, a photographers' magazine (in print form at least) tends to be extremely marginal, with reader figures in the low thousands. In Britain, Canada and Australia, a lucky few (for instance, 'Creative Camera', 'Ten.8', 'Image', 'Photofile', 'image nation', 'Source') have relied solely or occasionally on public funding. Mostly, editors get by as best as they can. In the early years of 'Creative Camera' its sole owner Colin Osman, offset the printing costs against his commercial publishing ventures; Carl Chiarenza, who worked voluntarily, persuaded his printer to shoulder some of the financial burden for a while. To save money while editing 'Album', Bill Jay moved into a flat with a friend. 'Reportage'

[6] This is based on the evidence of editorials that are carried in the inaugural editions of most photography magazines – the world around. The editorial from issue 1 of 'Ten.8', 1979, declares that it "was born out of the frustration felt by a small group of photographers working in Birmingham that the art was badly served in the area. Exhibitions are few and far between and many projects and individuals work in isolation, which is not deliberately self-imposed. That Britain's second largest city should lack a gallery is a profoundly unsatisfactory situation … a magazine was the most positive step we could take. We make no apologies … for starting from the area we know and working outwards, making connections as we go."
[7] Photography became of interest to general magazines almost immediately following its advent. Johnson, W.S. (1990). *Nineteenth Century Photography: An Annotated Bibliography 1839-1879.* California: Mansell..

owes its existence to a tax rebate. Such "narrowcast" publishing usually imposes comparatively low production values. On the other hand, editors of such titles enjoy an enviable level of autonomy because they are not answerable to either a powerful owner or advertisers, and this translates into loyal readerships. Publishers of photographers' magazines have included institutions, small presses, private individuals, but also commercial publishers. English 'Zoom' was one of those "core" titles identified by 'Afterimage' that was for-profit. Still, there is much room for disagreement about what should be classed as a photographer's magazine. What is a photographer anyhow? Throughout the fifties, sixties and seventies a typical "serious" photographer would be starved for information because few galleries displayed photographs and fewer critics reviewed photography exhibitions. Of course, those living in big conurbations were always likely to enjoy better access to whatever activities there were. For these reasons the photographers' magazines of that era aspired to be all things to all men, including a "portable gallery", an informal correspondence school about technique, history and taste, a place for exchanging ideas, a soapbox and even a token of belonging. In these years, during Modernism, readers were expected to take their cue from connoisseurs that intuited meaning from pure forms, equating it with the intention of an all-powerful photographer.

By 1980, following the advent of photography courses in higher education (in the US first), the aspiring practitioner would be better informed and less of a passive "reader" of images. Art photography was storming the museum, having acquired aesthetic credentials and a specific history (in 1979 'Creative Camera' listed nine current books about Stieglitz and promoted the Aperture Foundation's burgeoning History of Photography series of canonical monographs). No sooner had this consolidation taken place than critics and theorists began to emerge placing the premise behind this newest art form into contention (for instance Susan Sontag's 'On Photography' created ripples when it appeared in the US in 1977 and two years later in the UK). Such changes were reflected in the photographers' magazines of the moment, their diversity attesting to the increasing polarisation of the field into ever-smaller constituencies. While many titles defiantly continued the old "portfolio magazine" tradition of tastefully and expensively displaying images (the US and Australian periodicals, 'Picture' magazine, 'Photo Image', 'Light Work', 'Light Vision' among them), other more progressive titles addressed "critical" practitioners (US titles 'Afterimage' and 'The Dumb Ox' for instance), or those practising or interested in the social uses of photography ('Ovo' from Quebec), or indeed the "business" ('Photofolio' from the US and the bilingual 'Print Letter' focused on the growing phenomena of collecting, curating and so on). Prior to 1970, art photography had been a middle-class man's game, but the seventies witnessed a gradual, yet detectable, increase in women practitioners (image makers and writers). The advent of titles for feminist photographers, such as 'The Blatant Image' (US), and for left-leaning practitioners, such as 'Camerawork' (UK), demonstrated the compatibility of photography and politics. The trend towards audience polarisation and diversity has accelerated dramatically since the advent of e-magazines such as 'ZoneZero' and dedicated photography blogs such as '5B4'.

This book contains interviews with editors that were active (some still are active) prior to and since 1980, when magazine consumption appears to have peaked. The list of participants is by no means definitive, but rather random, reflecting a range of circumstances that affected my ability to make contacts. But I think it is representative. The interviewees include one current editor and nine former editors. They are predominantly male, reflecting the bias in the gender balance within the sector. In order to define the specialism of the photographers' magazine, I asked each about their motivations and functions. Editors come in two kinds. Lorraine Monk, James Hugunin, Derek Bishton and Colin Jacobson and are all "founder-editors". Carl Chiarenza, Bill Jay[8], David Hlynsky, Geoffrey Batchen and Richard West, on the other hand, are editors that took over from previous incumbents, meanwhile Jack Schofield assumed control of a franchise. While founder-editors possess a comprehensive understanding of their titles, editors, by contrast, usually perceive their achievements in relation to the legacies of previous editors. This means that, as a representation of a magazine, the interview with the founder-editor may be more accurate and satisfying. This, however, is not an option when a title has been edited by a succession of people. I was the seventh editor[9] of 'Creative Camera' during its 33-year existence and my version of 'Creative Camera' could be considered as a separate "text" from any of the other editors – not simply because the design and contents are different, but because every editor was required to respond to widely different circumstances and trends. A fairer representation of 'Creative Camera' – or any other long-lived title – would, of course, take into account the views of all editors[10].

Magazines are ideally placed to drive change argues David Abrahamson. In his essay, 'Magazine Exceptionalism: the Concept, the Criteria and the Challenge' [11], Abrahamson lists the characteristics that he thinks make magazines exceptional (as opposed to newspapers, for instance). Since the seventeenth century, he reminds us, they have aspired to shape, "the very social reality of their cultural moment." He writes: "the editorial content of magazines is specifically designed by its editors and looked to by its readers as something that will lead to action." All of the interviewees here expressed a desire to change something in their part of the world of art photography. 'The Dumb Ox' which was founded in the mid-seventies, included

[8] Jay was also founder-editor of 'Album' (1970-71) after leaving 'Creative Camera'.
[9] I count Peter Turner's editorship twice, once 1970-78 then again 1985-1990.
[10] While the name of a title may stay the same, every editor has their own agenda. For instance, some contributors to Mark Holborn's 'Creative Camera' of the early eighties expressed opposition to the modernist values of the title as it had existed during Bill Jay's editorship.
[11] Abrahamson, D. (2007). MAGAZINE EXCEPTIONALISM: The concept, the criteria, the challenge. Journalism Studies, Vol 8 (Issue 4), pp. 667-670.

photography within a broad editorial purview that encompassed conceptual art and theory. The editors used provocative humour and rigorous arguments to counter the prevailing conservatism of formalist art photography. Co-editor James Hugunin hoped: "to put forth an alternative critical voice..." During the sixties and seventies 'Image' championed neglected Canadian photographers. Its founder-editor, Lorraine Monk (who refuses to classify 'Image' as a magazine) supported photographers because they were uniquely placed to "show us what our country looked like, what our fellow countrymen looked like", yet were under-valued and under-exposed. During the eighties 'Ten.8' deployed photographic practices that addressed issues of ideology. Derek Bishton recalls the process by which the magazine transformed into "a vehicle for investigating lots of interesting ideas." In the nineties Colin Jacobson founded 'Reportage' with the intention of saving, or reviving the threatened art of the magazine photo-essay. He hoped his title would "continue that tradition ... of promoting self-contained picture stories that stand on their own."

Those interviewees that took control of existing titles made them into catalysts for change. In the late sixties Carl Chiarenza realized that photography was in danger of mirroring art history's entrenched habit of representing things as a dialectic of the new and the outmoded. Art photography, as he understood it, was the product of a confluence of ideas and he wanted his version of 'Contemporary Photographer' to reflect this. "You look at the past to understand and to develop from it, to build on it and expand it, not to shut it off... That's what we were trying to do with this publication". The contents of Volume V, No 4 illustrate Chiarenza's stated aim. Bill Jay, who began editing 'Creative Camera' around the time 'Contemporary Photographer' folded, waged a campaign to improve the standing of young art photographers within the moribund cultural institutions of the time. He states "...there was not a single gallery ... there was not a single museum in the whole of Britain which collected photographs as photographs... 'Creative Camera' attempted to change all that." In 1970 he established 'Album' to continue the "fight". In the mid-eighties Geoffrey Batchen recognised that the photography scene in his native Sydney was out of touch with trends in America, from which he had recently returned. Within a year he'd transformed the sleepy magazine, 'Photofile' into a forum for the latest postmodern writings and image making, provoking the ire of die-hard modernists. Batchen explains his intention was to use the magazine to shift photography "from its own ghetto into the broader cultural and artistic debates in Australia at the time". In the late seventies, during the enlightened Trudeau years, David Hlynsky took over a free sheet that was published by the radical Coach House Press in Toronto. Hlynsky wanted image nation to cover photography in a way that reflected its key role as part of the city's thriving arts scene. "The Information Age was about to dawn. Artists were gaining access to traditional print media and to video. So we made a magazine that celebrated the diversity of photography." The original mission of 'Source' photographic review, founded in Belfast the early nineties, was to promote and support marginalised Irish talent in photography institutions throughout the UK. Almost two decades later the magazine is still committed to this aim.

The putative subject of this book is the photographers' magazine, but it can also be read as a very partial (oral) history of photography by some of its most vociferous advocates in different parts of the world and at different times. These interviews address events that span approximately the years 1960 till the present. This volatile and vibrant period began optimistically with the consolidation of an autonomous (modernist) art of photography, then was followed by a phase of postmodern scepticism that in turn gave way to the "alter-modern" relativism of the present. Events from the mid-1990s have been dominated by the massive impact of digital technology on the one hand, and the implications of the selective recuperation of art photography into art history, on the other. The historical turning points, discursive spaces and debates that have arisen from photography as a result of these and other changes, are accessible in more and more books, mapped out and indexed for effortless consumption.

One of my aims was to provide the view from the engine room, so to speak, that would (at the risk of appearing anecdotal) restore some of the "static" that has been ironed out in the official record. These interviewees offer personal insights into events that motivated magazine producers, their contributors and readers. This includes Lorraine Monk's hair-raising accounts of her first photography exhibitions in Ottawa, in the sixties, as a "token female". Carl Chiarenza's impressions of life, first as a student of Minor White, then as a photographer and editor are amazingly evocative of an era in which a few photographers' magazines were unrivalled in their influence within their field. Even in the late sixties, it seems, the responsibility for writing the history and theory of photography belonged to ad hoc practitioners that were teaching themselves on the job. Chiarenza, who was one of these, offers a colourful picture of the new frontier that existed before photography won the attention of scholars. If anything seemed possible then it was because the rule book was still being written. The massive influence of French thought on photographic theory from the seventies is now a matter of dry textbook history – but how did it affect people at the time? The sheer power of new ideas to change lives as well as habits is reflected in Geoffrey Batchen's vivid memories of student life in Sydney in the mid-eighties. He recalls: "Your whole world view shifted as a result of reading that stuff." James Hugunin became so outraged by the intransigence of modernist pundits in the face of the new ideas, that he disrupted a lecture tour by a famous East Coast museum curator. Another vivid snapshot of photography during the transforming tide of postmodern theory is from Derek Bishton. He recalls how 'Ten.8' grew out of a meeting between alternative journalists and academics such as Dick

Hebdige and John Taylor (a major figure in the development of that magazine along with Rhonda Wilson).

The complex and often symbiotic relationship between the art and commerce of photography is a theme that pervades many of these interviews, and it is a subject that has so far evaded most historians. Colin Jacobson's painful memories of his growing isolation as 'Reportage' began to hit financial problems, sheds particular light on this, as indeed does Bill Jay in narrating the rise and fall of 'Album' in the early seventies. Commerce is also the subject of Jack Schofield's fonder recollections of his work at 'Zoom' in London in the 1980s. "Zoom was an image magazine, not a photography magazine," Schofield told me. The word "image", of course, has two meanings. Published in Paris, 'Zoom' loved sensational images and traded on its glitzy image. The magazine published old masters such as Lartigue, alongside the chic-est commercial photographers around, meanwhile its production values attracted the envy of rival photo editors.

These photographers' magazines mirrored and chronicled change but also sought to affect it. Did any of the editors actually achieve change via their magazine? The answer depends on who you ask. In his book 'Truth Needs No Ally', Howard Chapnick tells how the great Hungarian photojournalist André Kertèsz was finally recognised in the US, after years of neglect, in the 1968 exhibition, "The Concerned Photographer". According to Chapnick, Kertèsz's rehabilitation into the top ranks of photography started after "the famous editor" Romeo Martinez devoted a special issue of 'Swiss Camera' to him[12]. Is this true? Could it even be tested? Or is it more revealing of perceptions about the influence of these editors and their magazines? As David Abrahamson himself admits: "How to prove that one thing causes another? Did A cause B, or did B cause A? Or did C cause both A and B?"

Magazines are much misunderstood and comparatively neglected within the study of photography and there might be any number of good reasons for this. I hope this publication helps to remedy that situation. While there is growing interest in photographic books and pictorial magazines of various sorts, material about these magazines whatever they are called – is still sparse and relatively hard to find[13], partly I suspect because of the difficulties of classification I have alluded to. In the process of producing this book I stumbled upon useful or important material about magazines and editors that I have included in a bibliography section at the end. One of these is a survey of US "little" photography magazines of the East Coast written by A.D. Coleman. This excellent piece of research unexpectedly complements my interview with Carl Chiarenza. Likewise, I discovered

[12] Chapnick H. (1994) *Truth Needs No Ally,* Missouri, University of Missouri Press.

[13] The photographer's magazine has, however, benefited from a recent trend in photo publishing for facsimiles. In 2001 Steidl Verlag issued an excellent facsimile edition of the classic Japanese title 'PROVOKE'.

additional information about Lorraine Monk in a 1979 issue of the Canadian periodical 'Photocommuniqué'.

I am arguing that there is a type of magazine which addresses very specialised and discriminating communities of readers – which differs from the mass-market photography titles. The diversity within the photographers' magazine sector reflects the polarised nature of photographic constituencies. Editorial approaches may differ, yet there is a shared commitment to define and influence "the field". Edited by specialists, photographers' magazines represent a unique "insider" record of the shaping and reshaping of the borders of the art of photography over decades. This alone should be enough to make them worthy of investigation.

In conclusion, printed photographers' magazines have not, as was once supposed, vanished as a result of internet competition. On the contrary, the net offers financially hard-pressed editors a cheap and effective way to reach more prospective readers than ever before. Undoubtedly, the internet has encouraged a renaissance in magazine publications that promote the art of photography. These titles demonstrate many features in common with their printed counterparts, but differ in important ways too. For instance, editors of old-fashioned magazines are still held accountable in a way that those that run digital publications are not. But for me, the key difference between them lies with perceptions of loyalty. Readers of print magazines express their support by purchasing single issues or subscribing, providing a vital financial life-line. Support in the digital realm is about participating interactively, leaving useful comments after features or sending content for consideration. By trading "top down" editorial control for "bottom up" interactivity, editors of e-magazines seem to have conceded some of the authority that is still invested in the editors of printed magazines. For this reason, photographers still look to print for validation. And because printed magazines still offer a tactile engagement with images, valued by many photographers, there is every chance that they will continue to be an important feature of the scene for some time yet.

David Brittain

Contemporary Photographer

VOLUME V NUMBER 4

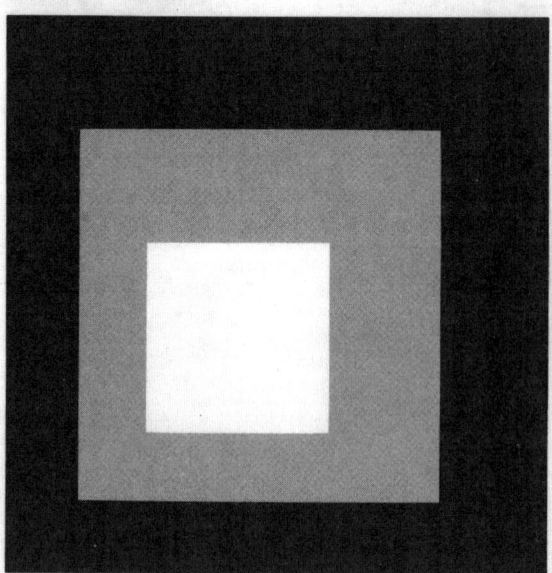

Carl Chiarenza: *Contemporary Photographer*

Founded in 1962, 'Contemporary Photographer' supported both photojournalists and art photographers and staunchly promoted the notion of an "independent photographer". The title, which was published in the New York area, folded in 1969. The photographer and educator, Carl Chiarenza, was editor for the last three issues, and prior to that, associate editor with Lee Lockwood.

David Brittain: What was the climate for photography around the time you began editing 'Contemporary Photographer' in the late 1960s?

Carl Chiarenza: Let me take you back to the mid-fifties when I was a student. There were 14 people in an overlapping class at RIT [Rochester Institute of Technology], including Jerry Uelsmann, Bruce Davidson, Ken Josephson, Pete Turner, and Peter Bunnell. The interesting thing about that moment was that both Minor White and Ralph Hattersley (both pretty unusual mentors) were teaching there. One of the many things where they were sort of at opposite ends of the spectrum over was the picture sequence. Minor was focusing on individual pictures or sequences and concentrating on the single image or the sequence of images as relating to each other without text – usually though he did some sequences with text as well. But the text was always on a separate sheet and was at the beginning or the end of the sequence... One of the things Hattersley was into is 'LIFE' magazine. So he's analyzing the public magazines. So we're getting stuff from both ends. It was the peaking of 'LIFE' magazine in the mid-fifties; Gene Smith is a major figure at that time – so we were very conscious of his arguments with the magazine over how to lay out a picture story, about how the pictures relate to each other and how does the way you put them together with text and captions help convey the emotions of the drama of that particular issue (whatever it might be ... "Schweitzer", say). So, we were being exposed to two different approaches to a similar idea about making and using photographs.

About Contemporary Photographer: Tim Hill was first editor and Don Patterson was second editor. Photojournalists were losing venues for their work ('LIFE', 'Look', 'Holiday' and other such magazines). So they were looking for places to do stories. That's one of the things 'Aperture' wasn't doing (it never really did). Everybody who was involved with 'Contemporary Photographer' was very conscious of Aperture and conscious of trying to bring something to the public (the 1200 people who saw these things!) that showed photography in a broader spectrum, but just as seriously treated. There's an issue of 'Contemporary Photographer' with Duane Michals and myself where you have independent pages, white borders and single pictures. They are sequences in a sense closer to what Minor [White] was doing, and then you have the [Charles] Harbutt documentary style article [Volume V, No 3]. Then you have the symposium that dealt with the problems of photojournalism in photography. We knew that 'Aperture' was a serious publication whether or not you agreed with it – it was serious and intense and it had a message. And we digested it thoroughly. At 'Contemporary Photographer' we were essentially trying to do the same thing (and that was true probably of 'Creative Camera' as well): to get the word out about what serious photographers were doing at that moment. But once you got going you did more than what you set out to do, in one sense, and less than you set out to do in another sense. I think 'Contemporary Photographer' was trying to be broader in terms of kinds of photography (that were being published). But it was so restricted by limitations: we didn't have the resources Minor had – either for printing or the resources of the community he had that was more established in terms of that kind of publication.

What sort of course was the one at RIT?

When we got there it was a two-year programme in applied photography – you learned chemistry, sensitometry and colour theory and optics and you did studio classes in portraiture and advertising; it was that kind of school. In the second year Ralph Hattersley formed the nucleus programme that became the bachelor of fine arts programme that we moved into from our second year. We moved into a third year that wasn't yet established when we came; and it involved Minor. So you can say that few of us came out doing what we went there to do . Most of us didn't know what the hell we were doing. We were students of photography and there was no place to go except RIT. I went there because it was the college I could afford. I was interested in picture making and photography; I lived in Rochester, I could go cheaply and probably thought I would end up working at Kodak. That's the kind of thing that happened to all of us. (Jerry Uelsmann came to RIT with the idea of opening a portrait studio!) To some extent that was true about all the stuff that happened at that time – opportunities arose and you moved into them.

In the early 1950s Aperture began a search for a critical discussion around photography. Tell me what your memories of that were around this time.

It begins with Beaumont [Newhall] and Minor, Ansel [Adams], Dorothea Lange, et. al. Minor ... from the very beginning ... was very clear that he was trying to develop a language with which to talk about photography. One of the things that made that clear, besides 'Aperture', was that he was working on a manuscript called "How to Read Photographs" which he gave me and Uelsmann and Bunnell and others to read and to respond to. That was based on Heinrich Wolfflin's book, 'Principles of Art History'. He tried to adapt Wolfflin's language to photography. Then Walter

Chappell came to town and he and Walter started working on this idea together. That exchange became that well known article published in 'Aperture' (Vol 5, No 3, 1957) – that was essentially about how to talk about photographs.

What did you think of that article in 'Aperture'?

I remember it well enough to know it was a very intriguing and interesting piece for us. It had, as all Minor's stuff had, that overtone that you've always got to sort of get beyond. But basically, it was an introduction to how to think about and talk about pictures, how to look at them; how to share what you saw or thought about with someone else by writing about it: by developing a language. You also have, at the same time, Henry Holmes Smith in Indiana who's engaged in a similar effort in his newsletter with much more down to earth language. And in fact the meeting of Smith and Minor, through 'Aperture', brings these two different kinds of languages together to begin to teach picture-makers as well as viewers how to make and experience photographs.

At the time did these ideas answer the need for a discussion?

There was an issue of 'Aperture' (Vol 5, No 2 1957) that came out of a famous assignment Minor gave that contained excerpts of writing about photographs, by members of our class at RIT. I sat in front of a Weston picture – I don't know if it was for an hour or two hours …

So how was that?

In some ways it was amazing. It certainly contributed to the fact that most of us students began to be more conscious of every detail as well as the whole; and thus, to make photographs more stimulating. I wrote a long piece on that Weston picture but it wasn't published in 'Aperture' – though 'Aperture' did include a poem and other excerpts that I wrote about other pictures. In fact, in print somewhere, I stated that one thing Minor had done for me – among many things is: he made me understand that a picture is everything that happens from edge to edge and from corner to corner within it; which is a natural result of long looking, thinking, responding, and writing critically.

The issue of "reading" pictures may have become confused because of Minor's insistence on encouraging people to read single images.

That was Minor's assignment and people talk about it endlessly. But at the same time he was talking about sequences. He was making sequences, we saw them, and we looked at them and we thought about them. I co-curated, with Davis Pratt, an exhibition at Harvard in 1968 that was called 'The Portrait in Photography' and in that exhibition we had Minor White's sequence (number 17 or 19). I asked him if I could put that in the exhibition and call it a self-portrait and he said, yes... I think that Minor did convey both ideas – the reading of one picture and of a sequence – because if you've studied a picture and you've understood that then you can understand how it is related to the next picture and then the next picture because you were so conscious of what was going on. It is related to what I was saying earlier about how to put together a Gene Smith story in a 'LIFE' magazine layout – they're different but they're very closely related.

Minor White seemed to be saying that an exercise for the maker of the picture is the reading of that picture in order to see if a feeling has been communicated – not that it is actually possible to communicate a feeling – but, for the success of the image, the reader is a sounding board. I don't think that's anything to do with critical thinking.

You're right to make a distinction between developing a critical language to be used by people who are going to be writing about the medium and the distinction between the photographer, him or herself, understanding what it is the photograph is. That's interesting because at that time there are no serious critics, there are no serious photography historians in the colleges or writing in scholarly journals – there's Beaumont Newhall and Minor trying to fiddle around with historical issues in 'Image' magazine[1] which Nathan [Lyons] later continued. The fact is – and it's true for my entire life – that I wrote criticism and history while continuing my picture-making career. With very few exceptions, photographers themselves produced almost all the writing that did happen. The few exceptions included H.H. Smith's newsletter, Jacob Deschin's 'New York Times' articles (and later, his own slim publication, 'The Photo Reporter'). Why I get confused in my own head is that I learned to write about pictures as a picture-maker, not as a historian: I did that later. I ended up being a historian – and that's another story, but I certainly didn't set out to do that. I supported making pictures by doing all those other things...

[1]Image magazine was published by George Eastman House.

Where was 'Contemporary Photographer' produced?

When Don Patterson took it over he was in Virginia then he moved to Boston and that's the way we became connected. Lee Lockwood, who preceded me as editor, was a photojournalist who was working out of the Black Star Agency based in Boston and New York. In those days there was constant travel between New York, Rochester and Boston. So one could say it wasn't really produced anywhere; it was produced in the air, in the mail or on the telephone. If there was a place it was Boston for the longest stretch. But the place was where whoever edited the issue was. The printing and mailing was centered in Culpeper, Virginia.

The printer funded it?

As you were asking the question I was trying to figure out who paid for the postage – it must have been the printer who was this unusual guy in Culpeper who I visited only couple of times. The magazine was printed there and I think that was arranged by Don Patterson (we called him "Pat"). Since Pat was from Virginia he probably made the connection with Culpeper Press. The printer, J.D. Wohlleben, had some kind of interest in doing it. He was the person who got whatever subscriptions/sales money came in (it went directly to him). None of us ever saw, or expected, a dollar or a cheque! The designer worked for free, everybody who wrote worked for free. The artists never received a reproduction fee. I'm sure even the printer lost money on the project.

Where did you get your mailing list?

I don't remember. It just grew over the years.

Aperture listed its subscribers.

Many of 'Apertures' readers were people who donated money. Though 'Aperture' also suffered heavy financial problems. We never had patrons. The mailing list eventually must have come out of the sources we had, which started out with the small community we all knew – perhaps Black Star Agency, ASMP, Magnum, etc. had loanable lists. Perhaps when the Society for Photographic Education [SPE] came into existence the membership list was used. SPE began with about 30 people in 1962; today it numbers about 2000. That reflects the changes in publications between then and now that we are discussing.

Do you remember the final size of your list?

I remember hearing, I think, that we reached a high of 1200. That was huge for those days.

Tell me about the transition from being associate editor (of 'Contemporary Photographer') to becoming editor.

Essentially, the way it happened was that Lee [Lockwood] was getting tired of producing it, and he was getting more assignments as a freelance photographer, so we did this issue (Vol V, No 3). Before this he asked me if I would take over. So we did this issue together and that was the transition. He got the Harbutt and Grey Villet portfolios. Lee obtained the letters from Japan. I produced the text. The writers were friends of mine: Ralph Hattersley was one of my teachers from RIT, Charles Millard is a close friend of mine, an art-historian, curator and museum director; we went to school together at Harvard. Pat Patterson (Donald Wright Patterson, jr.) was the second editor; the founder/editor/publisher was Thomas (Tim) Hill who did Vol 1, Nos 1 and 2. I don't remember whether Lee arranged Hill's article or whether I did. Of the others, Grace Mayer was associate curator at the Museum of Modern Art. Sam Edgerton taught with me in the art history department at Boston University. Lee arranged the article written by Tim Reynolds. So it was about fifty-fifty.

Your first issue as editor was Volume V, No 4. The text is different, both in its size and in its content, from that in the previous one, and I think even the feel for the text is different.

Lee was a photojournalist and New York-based. And I was more connected with the art world. In some ways it would have been better if we had continued together. Between us we had a larger contact with the world of photography. But that's the way it goes.

Why the change in format? It's now square.

I don't remember. I worked to redesign the whole thing with a friend, Bill McLane. Margaret Powell, who is listed as art director in previous issues, was Wohlleben's associate and the art director at the Culpeper Press. But William F. McLane designed Vol 4, and following issues.

This cover says 'Contemporary Photographer' and it has this "modern" design – like a meeting of design and typography. The motif could be a photograph but it might not be.

No, this cover does not include a photograph. It's more like an Albers' square. Bill did the whole thing. I am "guilty" of having chosen the contents as well. Marie Cosindas and Warren Hill [who were featured with portfolios] were both Boston photographers. Warren Hill and I founded Imageworks, which was a sort of version of the Visual Studies Workshop (VSW), but in Cambridge, Massachusetts. That existed for about three years, but we could not sustain the funding. While it lasted it was a terrific place; it had workshop classes. It had master students, the way the VSW had, and it had many workshop courses running throughout the year, and ran a regular series of exhibitions and lectures with people such as Duane Michals and many others. But it was costing one benefactor (Don Perrin, owner of Crimson Camera in Cambridge, MA) a lot of money. Imageworks was sort of replaced later by the Photographic Resource Center at Boston University which was spearheaded by Chris Enos and A.D. Coleman (and shortly after with help from me at the university).

This issue (Volume V, No 4) was important because it was the first time seriously alternate views were brought together – I'm talking about the pictures and the articles. They are all manifestos for breaking the rules. The rules had sort of been set up in twentieth-century photography from Weston and Adams (f64, previsualization, and zone system), and Strand and Stieglitz down, on to Minor [White] – all the rules that Jerry Uelsmann and Robert Heinecken (who were promoting manipulative techniques) were attacking in their articles (originally as SPE lectures) for this issue, essentially saying that there are other alternatives. And why aren't we looking at those. That was also true of Ralph Hattersley. So all that issue's writers are asking for something different. That was a point of view that I got from studying at the same moment with Ralph Hattersley and Minor White who were presenting opposite positions: both extremely creative teachers, but between them showing that there was a spread within the medium of potential and possibility; rather than one or the other. So this issue was an attempt to try to show alternative views.

Would you go along with A.D. Coleman's thesis that there was a conspiracy to enshrine "straight" photography at a high level at the expense of all other sorts?

Not a conspiracy, exactly. I came out of that tradition. The thing about our generation that is important I think, is that no matter what we, individually, were going to do (and I think Jerry Uelsmann and Robert Heinecken would concur with me on this) we never lost touch with the past; we never lost respect for the past. Even if we were going to challenge it – as Uelsmann did or Heinecken did in new directions – people never attacked the past in a way as to say that was stupid or dumb. Between the fifties and the seventies people were seeing their work as a progression or development, using what came from the past and building from it in different directions – which is what art is about. It's about moving in new directions but never losing sight of where it's coming from. At least that's my view of it. What's happened in the last twenty-something years is that many younger artists have sort of thrown the past away and are beginning "anew" with little sense of what they're using from the past. In the fifties to sixties in particular, young artists knew what they were using from the past and how they were building from it. Historians and makers were very conscious of the whole history of photography. That's, I think, the important difference between this kind of development from the past – in a new direction – and the major current thing which is just not to look at the past and to say, it's all bad (white European males and all the rest of that kind of political/ theoretical jargon) and in the process throwing out all the visual stuff. You look at the past to understand and to develop from it, to build on it and expand it, not to shut it off. So the features in this issue promoted developing new directions and promoted a respect for and understanding of the past. That's what we were trying to do with this publication: to show the range of the medium rather than narrowing it. We rarely suggested that there was something wrong with what happened before, but rather that there was more to be done. Evidence of this is supported by the writing of the time – almost all of the literature of import was written by photographers.

You believe the issue themed, "The Concerned Photographer" (Volume VI, No 2) was important. Why?

This was circa. 1966-68. I worked with Cornell Capa on this. It was essentially his idea. He was trying to promote the Fund for Concerned Photography, a fund that would provide money for concerned photographers at a point when photo journals (picture magazines such as 'LIFE' and 'Look') were dying. He was trying to find ways to continue supporting that kind of photography. The ICP in New York came out of this. He did a major exhibition and a catalogue about a group of those photographers. This CP issue came out before the exhibition and its catalogue (with the same title – "The Concerned Photographer" – as our issue) happened.

Was this the last issue?

Yes. The printer just said: we can't afford to do this any more, so we had to stop. A bit later I heard that Mark Power, a photographer in Washington, was going to become the new editor of 'Contemporary Photographer'. He had, I think, actually put together an issue with Wohlleben that had never come out. I don't know what happened. I edited three and one with Lee.

The first of your issues (Vol V, No 4) reflects more of your personal agenda. "The Concerned Photographer" issue was obviously something you felt needed to be done at the time.

Yes. It was an opportunity that I didn't think we should pass up. The editorial that I wrote about the conflict is very important to me; it's called, "Who cares: concern, protest, and action in photography." There was a struggle with Cornell over which pictures to use. I pretty much won. If you compare the pictures in this issue of CP with the pictures in Cornell's exhibition catalogue you can see that they are slightly different – I am always looking for a picture, which has many levels working, and Cornell tended to be more concerned with subject matter. That's an exaggeration but it's in the right direction. It's his selection of photographers and they are all major people. But I selected the specific pictures for reproduction. In different ways they all contributed... And working with Cornell was a great and unforgettable experience.

ICP has done wonders ever since. Cornell also participated in my group discussions leading up to the formation of Imageworks. We had another issue in the works with a couple portfolios including one by Ken Josephson. In fact that may have been the issue for which I asked Margery Mann to write. She later declined over an issue of feminism. A whole issue was planned, but we were not able to find funding for it. I became frustrated and stopped trying.

How would it have continued? Would you have kept broadening out the definition of photography?

Yes. I liked Ken Josephson's work, that, like Uelsmann's, was referenced to the past (to [Harry] Callahan in particular) but also moved in a completely new direction, that was beginning to open up the idea of a picture within a picture. That whole idea of appropriation is something Ken (and Robert Heinecken) already was doing, but quite differently from what came later. So that's an indication of what we wanted to do. It sounds a little weird saying it but I think the idea was to show how quality could exist in photography in different directions, and with different motives and purposes. We wanted to work with what the picture maker intended, did, presented. In the seventies I wrote an essay called "Toward an Integrated History of

Picturemaking", which was first given as a lecture in a series of lectures by various people called 'The new histories of photography' at the Art Institute of Chicago, and that really is where I was and still am. I think all pictures are related and there are quality productions in all these areas and what we should study is how they related and how they expand each other. The medium is much too expansive, too full to limit it; too broad for narrow restrictive theories driven by bias, by political motives.

You have said you were concerned about the critical writing in 'Contemporary Photographer' because everyone had to learn on the job. Did you see any change about the late 1960s in the expertise?

There just wasn't very much being said. It was a struggle to find somebody to do something. We were pushing people like crazy to write. But most picture-makers don't write; don't know how to write, don't want to write. And nobody else was interested. Once that transition happened the whole thing exploded. For better or for worse, or for both. Back then one could read, weekly, every book and every essay as it appeared. Since the seventies and the rise of the art market's interest in photography it has become today an impossible task to digest even a portion of what is published (or exhibited). What has happened still amazes us elders.

When did that happen?

Certainly it was developing by the mid to late nineteen seventies. Afterimage did some really terrific stuff in the seventies. That was where my first work on Siskind appeared and that's where that article I mentioned earlier 'Towards an Integrated History of Picturemaking' appeared. Very important writing began to appear in that publication in the seventies, eighties, nineties. And, with some ups and downs, it has continued to the present.

There is a sense with 'Contemporary Photographer' – missing at the time in Aperture – of trying to connect with what was going on, the issues.

It was an amateur attempt to try to do something none of us had any training in. Lee, an active photojournalist, had a closer connection to picture-publications than I did. I was involved with a publication that my wife edited, called 'The Liberal Context', in which, actually, we published some portfolios by photographers. That journal was published by the Unitarian Universalist Association, a hotbed of activity for leftist, liberal views in the sixties. I did the portfolios. One, for example, reproduced a Paul Caponigro image on the cover. The texts were not about art or photography; they were political. There was also 'The Boston Review of Photography' that published four or five issues. We used to call it 'BRP'. There was 'Choice' in Chicago for which Aaron Siskind was co-editor. It was a primarily a poetry magazine. Besides 'BRP' and 'Infinity', and the popular camera magazines, however, there were others: for example, Jacob Deschin's singular little publication, called 'The Photo Reporter'. He had earlier, as a camera columnist, reviewed photography exhibitions for 'The New York Times'. So he was making the transition from having been a camera columnist to paying serious attention to what was going on at the Limelight Gallery and elsewhere, primarily in New York City. There was Camera magazine from Switzerland, edited by Allan Porter. In the mid-seventies others as well – 'Creative Camera', and 'Album', both edited by Bill Jay in England. And, soon after: 'Print Letter', 'European Camera', etc., and others in Asia. Amazingly, they were all very different – even at that stage.

There were, of course, other publications that occasionally referred to photography, but there was very little else. It was a period when it was all very parochial; everybody, in what was, at the time, a small world, was trying to do something with what they had, with resources very limited, not only in terms of money (almost everyone worked for free on these publications), but also in everything else. As an editor you were delighted if someone sent you something in the mail that you could publish.

Lee Lockwood was passionate – as were you – and that is up front in this magazine.

There was no critical discourse but everything is grounded in personal experience. Pat Patterson, the second editor, had a house in Roxbury, Massachusetts in the sixties during the height of the civil rights movement. Roxbury was a black community – a ghetto. And he had a gallery in his house. At the same time he was editing CP he was showing, largely, photographs of civil rights protests and other political issues relevant of the time. He too was very passionate about what was going on in the world, what was going on in photography. We were all close friends. Anyone who was doing anything was just trying the best they could to get something out. If you got something published you were ecstatic. As editors, we were often frustrated because it was difficult to get anybody to write – not because they didn't want to do, but because most photographers did not write, and most writers on art were not interested in writing about photography. There was little motivation to write because there was almost no audience.

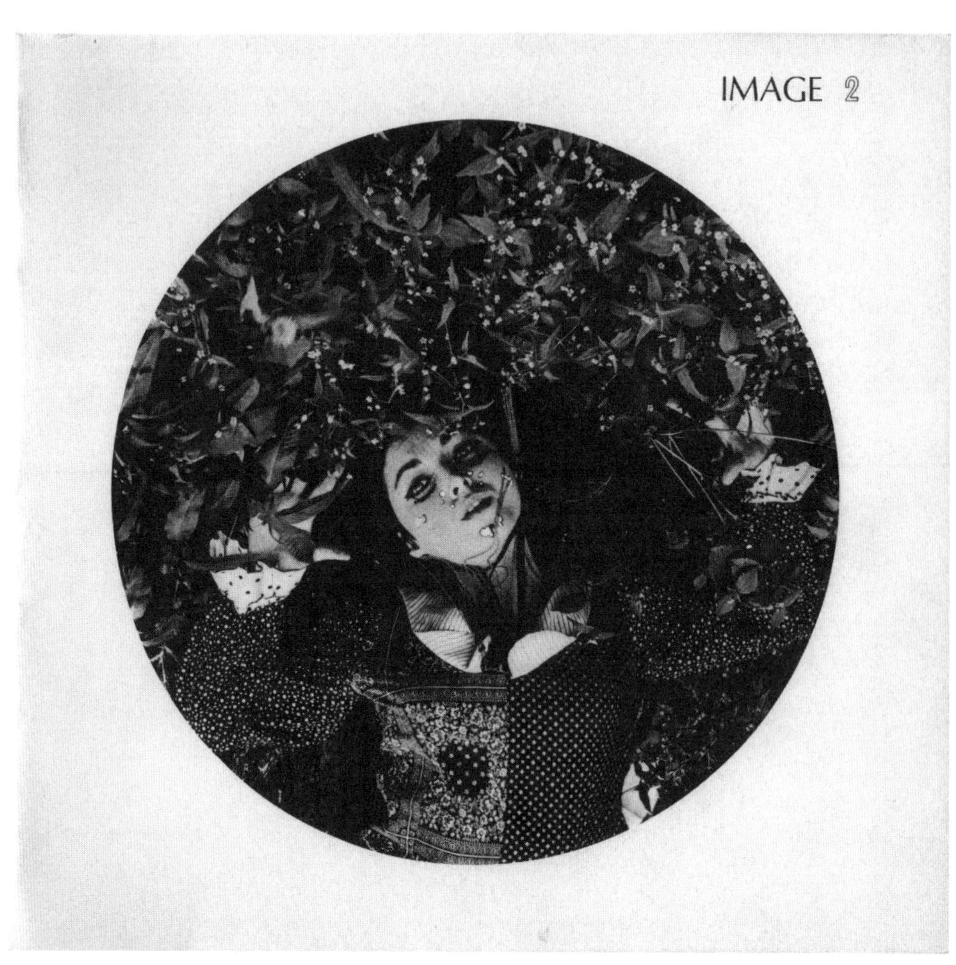
IMAGE 2

Lorraine Monk: *Image*

'Image' was a serial publication of the National Film Board of Canada. Whilst its primary function was to document the exhibition programme of its stills photography division, it also promoted Canadian-based photographers outside of Canada. The title ran between 1967-1971 consisting of 10 issues. Lorraine Monk was its founder and editor.

David Brittain: You were working at the National Film Board of Canada and also making exhibitions?

Lorraine Monk: It's possible you have the wrong idea about my work and the wrong person. I never edited a magazine.

OK, you call it a catalogue, but it was a periodical.

Let me tell you. Everything I did was illegal and I had no money for it okay; and so I had to sneak and cheat and lie and go underground to do everything I did. I was hired to do a particular job, which was to write. I was in Ottawa and the Film Board was in Montreal and they cared very little for still photography. I was able to do things because nobody knew what I was I was doing and nobody cared – that was what was important. I never had the budget to do anything and all this is going to do is encourage a lot of people to break the law and I don't think that's a good idea (laughs). I didn't edit anything, I didn't have any government backing, I didn't have a mandate for it, I did it because I felt the county needed it. And I also, I guess in a way, felt that I could get away with it. I was a woman and in government at that time – which was 99.99 per cent male – I was a sacred object – this token female and they're not going to fire a token female no matter what you do... And so there is great power in being a token female because you're untouchable. Everything I did was bizarre, against their rules. I was told: don't do it. I did it. I went into an empty space – not in a government building but a publicly-owned building in Ottawa – cleaned it up and put on a major exhibition, covered all the windows up; it had a metal grill ceiling and I got fishing line and big paper clips and I mounted the photographs onto Styrofoam and we stuck the clips into the Styrofoam and we hung them from the ceiling because one wall was all windows and one wall was doors with offices out of it and how are you going to hang it? And I asked all the VIPs in Ottawa – my minister, the minister of culture – all the diplomatic corps, black tie, and the next thing I know I've got the police trying to evict me. They couldn't evict me. The fire department came and were pretty adamant that it was a fire hazard – and it's very hard to stand up to a fire hazard; there aren't enough exits and there are too many people. Whereas the police say: you don't own this, you don't pay rent; it's owned by this person and you're a squatter and we're under orders to throw you out. And I said: well just try it...I did an exhibition every six weeks for 20 years – you know how many shows that is?

A lot.

It's a helluvalot. And I wanted to have a record of them, so I went to printers and said: how would you like to experiment, raise the bar? You pay for it. I wasn't editing anything. I did 200 shows and I ended up with ten 'Image' books, because first of all it's just too hard to be running around the country trying to get printers to do something for you when you have a staff of half a dozen people – most of whom are secretaries and file clerks. You're looking at this like someone in the Film Board set this up – they didn't.

How many would you print?

Maybe three to four thousand. And I gave them away.

You had no distribution.

We had no distribution. We had a price – $3.95 I think was the price for them – and we tried to sell them but we gave them to photographers who went through our offices. First of all, if you charge you eliminate all the students who don't have a nickel. I mean young people didn't have $3.95 in the sixties – our first show was in 1967. A lot of photographers in Canada were draft dodgers from the Vietnam war and were illegally in Canada. I hired them all and did shows of their work and gave them an 'Image' book. It had no structural foundation, no government money. I spent money I didn't have, I spent other people's money and finally when the treasury board called me onto the carpet – like whoever would have sentenced Essex to have his head cut off in England – to explain why I was doing so many illegal things, I went to the head of the treasury board and said: this is what I do, this is why I do it, and they won't leave me alone. Then I went to Trudeau and I went to the head of the privy council – and those three people said: leave this woman alone. So it had no normal structure, no funding or anything.

Why did it stop?

Because I moved here [Toronto]. After twenty years it had become very powerful. We'd done a lot of books. I did 'Between Friends/Entre Amis' (1976) – I got one and a half million dollars from Trudeau to do our gift to America for their 200th anniversary. I just wanted money to give to photographers … I wanted half a million dollars for photographers to go out and shoot – and they were desperate for money. Not to do commercial work, but to be free to express themselves in what they really wanted to do. And so I did get that money. But normally I just didn't have any money at all and I owed money everywhere and then defied the Film Board to fire me for running up debts of half a million dollars here and there. After five years of threatening eviction from this place we were squatting, I approached the head of the Treasury Board – you know how important that office is? (I made the mistake of saying, I've come to bear my breast: that got him listening to me). I told him why I was there, that the photographer was the low man on the totem pole, nobody gave a damn about them, and how important they were to show us what our country looked like, what our fellow countrymen looked like – essential national identity thing! After listening to me – the head of Treasury Board – he phoned a week or so later and said, OK Lorraine today I signed a special order in council giving you the right to that space in perpetuity. And I said, Gee Al that's really nice but you know it's such a little space and it's in the wrong place. He said, Lorraine I'm leaving to go and head up the CBC, you tell that to my successor! ... So it's not a normal story and I never edited a magazine in my life – 200 shows and ten 'Image' books.

How did you decide which shows got the books?

I would try and find a printer – a fellow in Montreal, who wanted to do gravure, came to me, saw the other Image books, and told me it was good advertising for them, good promotion and they liked dealing with photography. But they'd often do it after the show was down. There was no programme, it was all hit or miss. Then I wanted to do bigger books, and one day – they were all illegal – I got a letter from the Film Board in Montreal saying, we have now discovered that you are engaged in the production of 'Image' books, there are ten of them, and it said: as of today's date you will cease and desist and never again produce an 'Image' book. They were wonderful because photographers loved to see a record of their work. They were, for the most part beautifully printed and very important to photographers...When I got that letter I went into the most awful pout, sulk, depression – all of the above – but I sat in my office thinking: how do we deal with this one. I went out to my secretary and I said: read that to me. She read it. It said: cease and desist and never again produce another book. I said, Madeleine, as of today we produce a new series called Signature. And the Signature thing [a series of books featuring the work of Canadian photographers produced between 1972-1977] came out of our defiance of the Film Board. So this is not what you're looking for.

I am interested in how these publications came about.

Illegally and in defiance!

What was your role in the 'Image' books? Did you do the sequencing for instance? Did you liaise with the designer?

I did everything. A catalogue is a catalogue, there's not a lot of text in it. I sometimes wrote the introduction. And at one point I got Gene Youngblood who was at that time an important writer – but we didn't have any money to pay writers. And we were not publishing a magazine that would have any prestige for them to be in it. People wrote for nothing because they liked what I was doing running around like old mother Hubbard with an empty cupboard... We did start to make a big impact on printing quality and to win awards, but that never impressed anyone at the Film Board in Montreal – they never gave a damn.

The 'Image' book changes at some point – it seems to go from being a catalogue to becoming autonomous.

Which ones?

The issue with Pierre Vinet (9, 1971), Gregoire (7, 1970).

My boss was a homosexual and Pierre Vinet was a homosexual, and in those days you were not open about it. It was something to cover up... I was told by my boss to do that book. He wanted it and he got it. But you're dealing with such a unique structure and background that you're not going to be able to draw any conclusions from anything. Apart from that one, they were all shows.

All the photographers were Canadian?

Yes. Our mandate was that we would show Canada to Canadians and to the world (the Film Board mandate).

This remit – for Canadians to show Canada – applied to documentation and some of the work published in 'Image' was not documentation.

I don't think anyone in Montreal gave enough of a damn and we were in Ottawa. They were so involved in their own projects...

3s 6d December 1969 75c USA

creative camera

PHILIP JONES GRIFFITHS photographs from Vietnam
DANNY LYON destruction of Lower Manhattan
AGATHE GAILLARD photographic postcards
AARON SCHARF talking about explosions . . .
LEWIS W. HINE things to be appreciated
VAN DEREN COKE la daguerreotypomanie
ROBERT FRANK letter from New York

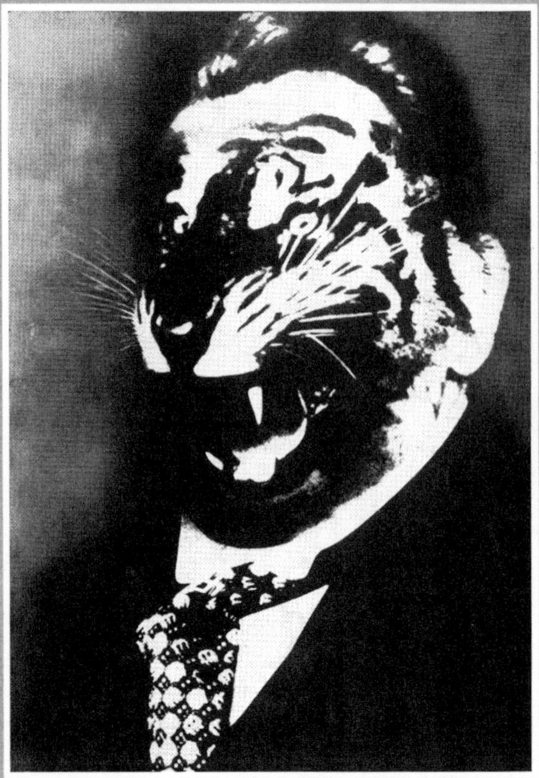

photo. John Heartfield

Bill Jay: *Creative Camera 1968-69 and Album 1970-71*

'Creative Camera' was founded in London in 1968 and finally closed in 2001. Under its first editor, the English writer Bill Jay, the title made a transition from a "hobby" magazine into the outspoken and influential advocate of the new British photography. After a year, Jay left the magazine to found and edit the short-lived 'Album'.

David Brittain: Can you describe broadly the British context in the 1960s as it appeared to you and photographers. I would include movies, design, the Sunday supplements, art, the alternative press and so on.

Bill Jay: Even though I was still in my twenties, I missed out on much of the Swinging Britain phenomenon. I was in a "difficult" marriage, with two small kids, living in the country (Cookham). If something did not directly involve photography then I probably missed it! Of course, I scanned every colour supplement, 'LIFE' etc., but only for photography. The only movie I remember was "Blow Up" which included images by Don McCullin and Sam Haskins. Incidentally, I was a frequent visitor to Haskins' studio (where "Blow Up" was filmed). Art? Jim Dine, David Hockney, Richard Hamilton... Design? *Nada*...To set the scene, back in the mid-sixties, there was not a single gallery in the whole of Britain regularly showing serious, non-commercial photography; not one ... there was not a single museum in the whole of Britain which collected photographs as photographs, other than as documents of fashion, architecture or whatever... the Institute of Contemporary Arts had not exhibited a single show of photography, as far as I am aware; there was not a single agency, organization, council or company which provided grants to photographers for the pursuit of excellence in picture making; the Arts Council of Great Britain would not even consider applications from photographers for several years; there was not a single photographic magazine in Britain which emphasized non-commercial, non-how-to-do-it, portfolios of images by committed photographers; photography as "art" elicited snickers of embarrassment if not downright incredulity; schools of photography which included any aspect of the personal approach to picture-making as a part of its regular curriculum were rare (Guildford School of Art was an exception, especially when under the iconoclastic leadership of Ifor Thomas, an educator way ahead of his time); there were no workshops where young photographers could learn from accepted fine photographers; there were precious few lectures by famous photographers – I cannot remember a single one during the first year of 'Creative Camera's' production; there was no market at all for the sale of original prints to collectors; the notion of paying even £20 for a photograph, even by a well-known photographer, was considered a ludicrous idea.

That's the bad news: the institutional foundations of photography in Britain were inert, inept and apathetic. 'Creative Camera' attempted to change all that and light a fire under their collective rear-ends. I am being deliberately offensive here, because that was how we felt: offended. And if this remark is also reminiscent of sixties anti-establishment rebellion, that too is appropriate. That's also a part of the Zeitgeist; that's who and what we were. In retrospect, and from the perspective of a more mellow, inclusive age it also sounds a bit pompous. And there was a tinge, say it ever so softly, of such conceit. We wanted to change the world, or at least that part of it that we most cared about – photography. A very important, and usually neglected, aspect of this revolutionary zeal was that it did not spring out of nothing. There was a small but cohesive group of professional photographers, based in London, who were alert to and engaged in the very best of international image making... They may not have enjoyed any institutional support but they were not without their own networks. In fact the lack of official respect and sanction made these networks even stronger and more vital.

The interchange of issues, ideas and images among these photographers was facilitated in several ways. And the most important of these occurred within the magazine and publishing world...

How did you find out what was happening outside the UK?

Books, for example, were major sources of knowledge and inspiration. Since the publication of the 'Family of Man' catalogue (1955) – to take an arbitrary starting point – there was a small but steady stream of fine photography flowing into Britain that the whole photographic community could share as talismans of merit. By this time, most British photographers of any seriousness already owned important books of images by Edward Weston, Ansel Adams, Paul Strand, William Klein, Walker Evans, Robert Doisneau, and many others. Even on a meager income, it was possible to acquire every worthwhile picture book on serious photography. To name just a few, published in the decade leading up to 'Creative Camera': 'Observations', Richard Avedon; 'The Americans', Robert Frank; 'Photographs', Aaron Siskind (all 1959); 'Moments Preserved', Irving Penn (1960); 'Perspective on Nudes', Bill Brandt (1961); 'Ordeal by Roses', Eikoh Hosoe (1963); 'The Painter and the Photograph', Van Deren Coke (1964); 'A Way of Seeing', Helen Levitt (1965); 'Every Building on the Sunset Strip', Ed Ruscha (1966); 'House of Bondage', Ernest Cole (1967); 'The Bikeriders', Danny Lyon (1968). And there was always the "bookends" of the photographer's shelf: 'The Decisive Moment', Henri Cartier-Bresson (1952), and 'Shadow of Light', Bill Brandt (1966).

...Like books, exhibition catalogues (usually imported from the USA and many featuring the curatorial work of Nathan Lyons) provided British photographers with another access to what was going on internationally. We were very aware of every major exhibition at the Museum of Modern Art, New York, and of the issues raised by its curators, John Szarkowski and Peter Bunnell, through the catalogues' articles, several of which were published in 'Creative Camera'...

In addition, the early colour supplements of 'The Sunday Times', 'The Observer', and 'The Daily Telegraph' were also publishing work such photographers as Lee Friedlander. In the same way, fine international photographers were regularly seen in 'LIFE', which stopped weekly publication in 1972; 'Look', which folded in 1971; 'Queen', which regularly assigned major features to Marc Riboud, Bruce Davidson, Brian Brake among similar photographers; 'Paris Match' and many other international picture magazines which were eagerly scanned by involved photographers.

And do not forget the year books published by periodicals such as 'Photography' and the 'The British Journal of Photography'. During the late 1950s Norman Hall, the editor of the former, was a true prophet of photography, a lone voice and a harbinger of things to come. He regularly published the work of then-unknown but later-acknowledged great photographers. That was even more true in his remarkable annuals. The Photography Year Books...

In Europe we looked to the fine Swiss magazine, 'Camera', edited by an American, Allan Porter, which showcased the best of ink reproduction available at that time and also published portfolios of fine photography of the past and present. I should also mention Photokina, held every two years in Cologne. Although primarily a trade show, it always included a cultural section of exhibitions, often by some of the best European photographers, organized for 20-plus years by Fritz Gruber, and accompanied by a handsome catalogue for those who could not attend in person.

Before leaving the topic of photographic periodicals, I must mention the most important one of all – and its title might come as something of a surprise: 'Popular Photography'. True, this magazine carried a surfeit of advertisements, then as now, and its main readers were techno-amateurs, but consistently, throughout the nineteen fifties and sixties, it published the most in-depth and comprehensive features on the greatest photographers. They remain some of the most important essays ever written about the major figures in the medium (and should be collated into an anthology).

... America was certainly experiencing the beginnings of a photographic upheaval in the early 1960s but its magnitude has been greatly exaggerated – as has its influence on 'Creative Camera' in 1967-68. The truth is that the current emphasis on fine-art photography in the USA was just beginning. Let's take the year 1963... Only one university offered a Master of Fine Arts degree in photography. By 1972 there were 59 MFA programmes...
Also in 1963, Norbert Klebert opened the Underground Gallery in the basement of his home in New York City. When Tony Ray-Jones and I arrived in 1968, it was still the only gallery (outside the Museum of Modern Art) devoted to serious photography – and even then it was only open at weekends and at night because Norbert was working full-time at a camera shop...

America was not so far advanced in its patronage of photographers. The National Endowments of the Arts fellowships began in 1967, just as 'Creative Camera' was getting started. More of the same would be tedious, but I wanted to emphasize that: 1) yes, institutional photography was a little more active in the USA than in Britain in 1968 but, 2) no, it was not as active as you might have been led to think. And, yes, we were well aware of what was going on.

Please tell us the "creation story" of 'Creative Camera'? How you became editor.

Since 1959 I had been writing regularly for practically all the photographic journals as well as any other interested periodicals. One of the photo-magazines to which I occasionally contributed was called 'Camera Owner'. It was edited by Jurgen Schadeberg, a fine photojournalist who had worked with Tom Hopkinson in the great days of 'Drum' in South Africa. But 'Camera Owner' was nothing like 'Drum'. It was sold through subscription leaflets enclosed with the packet of prints which snap shooters picked up from the local chemist. It offered tips on how to photograph your pet or child; it was aimed at such a photographic novice that writers were told they could not mention f/ numbers for fear of confusing the readers. I wrote the occasional article for Jurgen – and even got paid now and again, if I remember rightly. One day Jurgen told me he was fed up with the chore of producing a monthly magazine and that he was quitting. So I stepped into the job, more or less by default. It was not long before the publisher, Sylvester Stein, said the magazine was folding. Intrigued, I told him I had always wanted to edit my own magazine if he wanted to give it to me. I had no money and even less chance of acquiring any. While I was still pleading with Stein, a fairy godmother walked into my life, in the unlikely form of Colin Osman.

Colin already published a successful journal for racing pigeon fanciers. After Colin had paid Stein one pound for the magazine's name, we walked back to his offices on Doughty Street and there, to the cacophony of cooing pigeons, began a partnership which led to 'Creative Camera', Colin was publisher; I was editor.

The immediate problem was how to radically change the editorial content of the magazine without instantly disenfranchising the snap-shot subscribers. We decided the change had to be gradual. Over a period of months the magazine moved away from snap-shot appeal towards serious photography, and the name changed from 'Camera Owner' to 'Creative Camera Owner', to 'Creative Camera'. By January 1968, the editorial contents were on track.

Only one other problem remained: our intended supporters – serious photographers – were too few in number to keep the magazine afloat... In the end I was forced to take full-time jobs, as European Manager of Globe Photos, an international picture agency, and as Picture Editor of 'The Daily Telegraph Magazine'. Both jobs were short-lived; 'Creative Camera' was my top priority.

Without the constant injections of aid from Colin Osman, 'Creative Camera' would have folded within months. That it survived for more than 25 years is due largely to his early generosity and enthusiasm...

These were frustrating, exhilarating, frantic times. There's nothing like fighting for a cause to get the juices flowing. We tilted at windmills and felt vindicated when they, in indifference, did not fight back. We provoked and attacked photographic schools, the Royal Photographic Society, other publications. The Arts Council, the Institute of Contemporary Arts, et al. Our constant hammering did seem to dent their armour on occasion, and in a few cases breached their defenses altogether. Such successes vindicated our goals, but led to an unforeseen problem: how could we practise what we preached without stretching our meager resources to breaking point..?

> The images in 'Creative Camera' were always raising hackles. It is difficult today to believe that our use of Jerry Uelsmann images prompted a barrage of abusive letters and verbal attacks. What was particularly galling about this was that I did not personally like Uelsmann's images – but I did believe they were important enough to publish. Inadvertently, we were causing conflict with every issue. We were even charged with obscenity – the offending photograph was of two nautilus shells by Edward Weston!
>
> ... Inhaling the Zeitgeist of the energetic sixties, photographers, like all other aspects of society and culture, were beginning to question established values and traditions. Individuality and self-expression were the rallying cries. Nothing was sacred or could be taken for granted. Radicalism was not a political slogan but a state of mind. In spite of the recent inevitable backlash and the not always healthy fallout of those attitudes, there was an excitement in the air that was invigorating. In that sense 'Creative Camera' was challenging, even attacking, the photographers of the era who were locked into a narrow notion of what constituted "photography."

You and Colin were different yet complementary in ways. How would you define the relationship at 'Creative Camera'?

> The relationship with Colin was prickly. I saw a distinct sharp divide between editor and publisher. Colin constantly wanted more editorial say. I refused. This led to increasing acrimony and eventually to him firing me.

Reading the 'Creative Camera' you edited now, one senses it is pulling in two directions at once – there's a focus on back-filling the history of photography: as art, as media, as a sort of folk art and so on, and then there's a concern with contemporary work, the media. Does this reflect the personalities/passions of two different editors (Jay and Osman)? Or was there just too much for such a magazine to do?

> Not in two directions – in scores of directions! This was not a reflection of two different editors, say Jay and Osman, because there was only one editor (me). I was adamant (or call it pig-headed, whatever) that I was the sole decision-maker as regards to content. As to why the contents seem so broad, this was (rightly or wrongly) my deliberate decision: to reflect the medium's past as well as present, its social/cultural presence, its links to other arts, its art and its artisan roles, etc., etc.. It was eclectic, scrappy, reverential and rebellious, I hoped. None of these roles were reflected in other British photo-mags, so I wanted to provide samples/tastes/tidbits of all that photography had been, was and could be. Personally, I was (and

still am) interested in all aspects of photography; in that sense 'Creative Camera' was a reflection of my own interests. If I was interested in an image, idea, essay or item then I presumed others would also be interested – and into 'Creative Camera' it went!

You were a word-oriented editor more than a picture-oriented one?

For me this is still an impossible question to answer. If I like historical photographs as images I feel compelled to conduct research into who, why, where, how, etc.; if I am intrigued by a contemporary image, I want to talk/write about it; if an issue arises – e.g. morality – I want to examine images as well as words and not only in the field, but also in politics, culture, society, history, etc.. I can't separate ideas (words) from emotions (images), they are inextricably intertwined.

Who was the 'Creative Camera' reader around the time you left?

No idea! I hope they were young and committed photographers who derived support and encouragement from examples in its pages. But this is pure speculation.

Just explain again the "creation story" of 'Album'.

In the Autumn of 1969, over a pint of bitter at the local pub, Colin Osman informed me that I would no longer be the editor of his magazine, 'Creative Camera'. By this time the magazine had become "his" in reality. Although I initially had 51 per cent of the company, I was obliged to sell Colin my shares in exchange for a small monthly allowance until I had nothing left. Our relationship had grown increasingly testy over the preceding year and, in retrospect, I can see why my goals for the magazine, and the way I was incorporating them, were causing friction. Colin first wanted, then demanded, greater editorial control. I did not respect his image judgments and refused. In the end, I prepared each issue and sent it for publication before he could see it and fight about its contents. This caused tensions, not surprisingly. At the time, however, I was too young, brash, and committed to notice or care. Still, the parting was traumatic. There was nothing I wanted to do more than edit a magazine in which I believed, heart and mind. So I wanted another magazine, badly, although I had no prospects or reasonable hope of ever getting one. But I dreamed of it...

Following my ouster from 'Creative Camera' the cosmic kaleidoscope had been shaken and the fragments were realigning themselves into a new pattern. The most important new element was Tristram Powell. He was a BBC television director and producer, son of the novelist Anthony Powell ('A Dance to the Music of Time'). I did not know any of that at the time; I presumed that when he telephoned he wanted me to see his photographs or publicize his latest movie. Over lunch he made a remarkable offer: he had £4,000 to "lose" and wanted to sink it in a fine photographic journal, was I interested? I was ecstatic. Over many meetings I came to respect Tristram for his intellect, generosity and cultivated demeanour. He advised, never controlled, and he was the perfect socially-priviledged gentleman of the arts to my working-class aggression. He has never received due acknowledgment for all his quiet, behind-the-scenes activism during this volatile period in British photography.

We were joined by Aidan Ellis, a young accountant at Colin Osman's publishing company, whose job would be to keep track of the money; an aspect of publishing with which I had little interest and even less acumen. Incidentally, I recently scanned the articles of association, which formed 'Album' (incorporated on 21 January 1970), and noticed to my surprise that the only shareholders were Tristram and Aidan. I was not included, although for all these years I had presumed I was an equal partner. Which just indicates how much attention I paid to the business side of things. By now I was fully engrossed in preparing the first issue.

At this point I received a remarkable offer from another backer who promised a far more financially secure future for me and for 'Album'. I declined. I had already committed myself to Tristram and Aidan. Do I have regrets, even now? Yes. I felt I was doing the honorable thing by keeping a promise made. But in my heart of hearts I wonder what could have been...

We moved 'Album' into a cheap damp basement, featuring flaky plaster and exposed pipes, at 70 Princedale Road, London W11. It was furnished with old benches, stools, a typewriter and, most important of all, a stuffed couch and a five-gallon jug of rough cider, more frequently used by the local tramps than our "guests"...

The first major decision we made about 'Album' was, in retrospect, the major eventual cause of its demise. We decided to spend more than one half of our total assets (Tristram's £4,000) into mailing actual first issues to more than 1000 individuals across the world. The idea, more optimistic

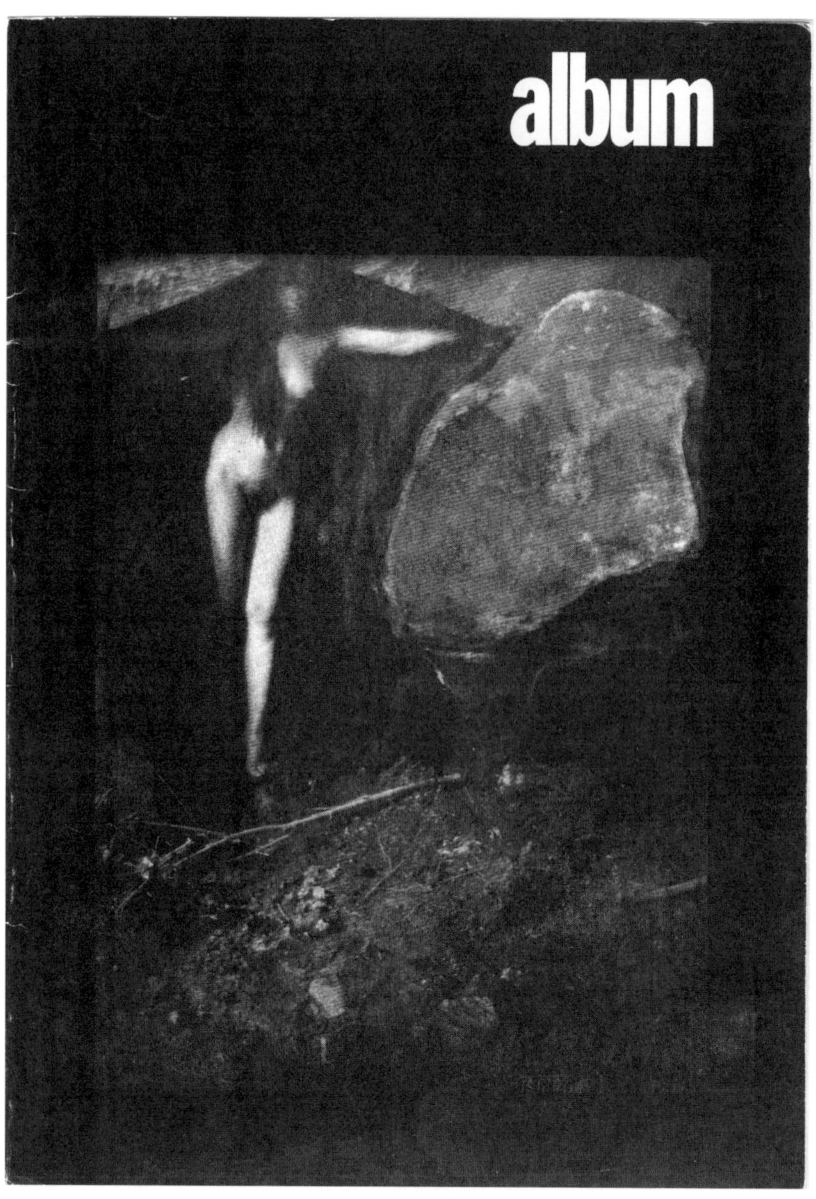
album

than realistic, was that if these people saw the first issue, most of them would subscribe, meaning that we would break even immediately. Such faith! Such naivety!

... Nothing, however, could shake our excitement, as we packaged the spanking new first issues in their envelopes and mailed them to names and addresses "borrowed" from lists supplied by the George Eastman House, Museum of Modern Art and elsewhere. How eagerly we picked up the mail, expecting to be flooded with subscriptions; how disappointed when they trickled in, in dribs and drabs.

Tell us about the end of 'Album'. What did it achieve?

... On the editorial side, I was in seventh heaven, collaborating with photographers such as W. Eugene Smith, Tony Ray-Jones, Thurston Hopkins, Cas Oorthuys, Les Krims, Imogen Cunningham, Emmet Gowin, John Claridge, Andrew Lanyon, George Rodger, David Hockney, Manuel Alvarez Bravo, Patrick Ward, Edouard Boubat, Elliott Erwitt, Don McCullin, Naomi Savage and the list goes on. I was producing a magazine that I would want to buy, the only editorial policy I ever had... Now, a glance through the pages of 'Album' releases memories of so many people and their generosities that it would need a book to give them full credit. But what is evident is that there was so much to do and a finite amount of time and money that my resources were stretched way past breaking point.

By the tenth issue of 'Album' it was very evident that we were sinking financially. If we were going to have any hope of breaking even, then drastic steps would have to be taken. The time between issues was increased (even though 'Album' was a monthly) in order to allow more new subscriptions to cover our printing bills; Aidan Ellis was asked to leave at this time, which saved us money but there were growing rifts between us leading up to this decision – like Colin Osman, Aidan wanted more editorial input, and I refused to give it to him; and we had to abandon our basement in order to save rent and utilities. 'Album' was homeless.

Learning that 'Album' was homeless, David Hurn said, in his nonchalant way, "why don't you move in?" So I did. Even though my presence – not to mention the constant ringing of the door bell by potential contributors, the endless cups of tea, the tying up of the telephone, the piles of prints and packing, the space commandeered for layouts, and the general hubbub – must have caused immense inconveniences in someone's home, David, never once, gave me the feeling that I was other than wholly welcome. And I will never forget the conversations and print-sharing among David, Patrick Ward, Don McCullin, Ian Berry, Elliott Erwitt, Charles Harbutt, Leonard Freed or whoever happened to be there. They are cherished moments in my life.

In the Spring of 1971, Britain was in an economic slump. Belts were being tightened everywhere – including at our printers. Balding and Mansell were not only handling all our income but had given us a three-month grace period in our bills. In essence we owed them for the printing costs on three issues. During the financial squeeze they had no choice but to take full payment. It wiped us out.

What did it achieve? Ironically, I think that the other activities – lectures, ICA photo study centre, etc. – had more of an impact on the next phase of British photography than the magazine itself. On the positive side, I think (or hope) that 'Album' was more instrumental in focusing the attention of the outside world on what was happening in British photography; e.g. A 'New York Times' essay (20 September 1970) about our activities that called me a "revolutionary". But who knows?

BILL JAY
5027 Santa Monica Ave, #E
San Diego, CA 92107

19 Jan. 05

Dear David

Many thanks for the text. It reads just fine – good job. Just a few corrections: p.7 "something" cc? omit p.7. The editor's name was John ANSTEY, not y; p.13 examples, not "d". Minor, and I'm sure you have already caught them.

As to publication, a small photo-magazine out of Washington state, *LensWork*, has asked to reprint the whole thing in a future issue, but no firm plans as yet.

By the way, where/when were you planning to publish your own pieces? A book, I think you said. Do you have a title, publisher? I would love to know. What is the book about?

It was good to regain some contact with you and I hope we keep in touch.

Best wishes

Bill

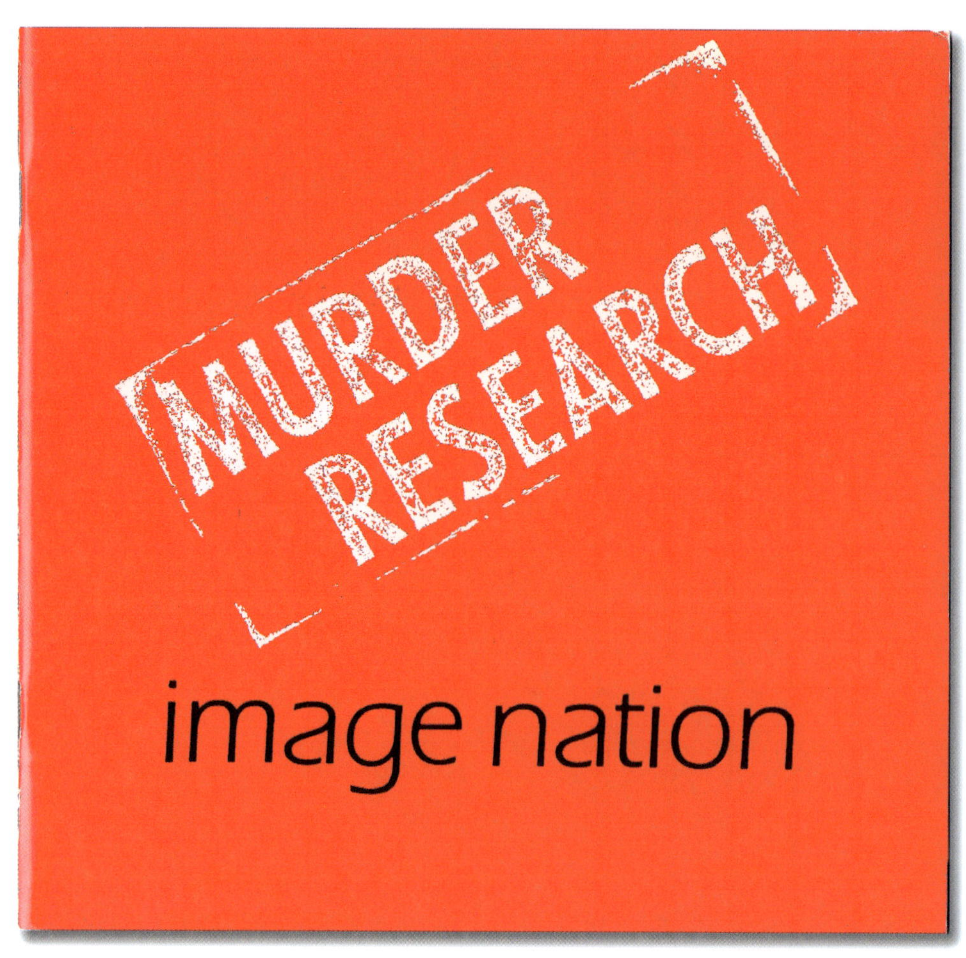
MURDER
RESEARCH
image nation

David Hlynsky: *image nation*

The vibrant and experimental photography scene of Canada in the seventies is chronicled in the pages of ‘image nation’, produced in Toronto by Coach House Press. Its editor, between 1973 and 1983, was the American artist and writer, David Hlynsky.

David Brittain: Summarise your history in magazines.

David Hlynsky: I attended art school at Ohio State University. There was no photography programme within the art department as Abstract Expressionism still reigned... Pop was just catching hold and Conceptualism hadn't caught our attention. This was also the time of the Vietnam war and the hippie generation. Our aesthetic was an odd mix of hippie romanticism, hard left politics and psychedelic Surrealism. We made photo illustrations that expressed those values and also subscribed to the school of 35mm black-and-white street photography. In 1971, I moved to Toronto and began to work at Coach House Press, a small literary publisher. 'image nation' had evolved from a newsletter for an alternative (free) university (Rochdale) and had become a photo arts showcase. I took it over after three photo issues.

In the seventies the British began setting up a support system for photography of publications, grants, galleries and so on. Did Canada have any support structure?

Yes, during the Trudeau era there were quite a few initiatives and grants aimed at cultural development. Many of these have survived and matured into bureaucracies today. A keystone in this development was a large network of regional "artist-run" galleries, production facilities and magazines. These continue to be born, evolve and flourish today. The contemporary Canadian art scene is many magnitudes more complex and active today even as the original cultural bureaucracy becomes more constrained. Festivals, galleries, publications, theatres and the like are now recognized as having a positive impact on Canadian life.

Am I right in thinking that in Canada practices reflect regional differences?

It's important to understand Canadian geography. Canada is the second largest country on earth after Russia. Our population is roughly 30 million, located mostly in the South and this makes most of our closest neighbour, America.

US cultural influence is dynamic and relentless. If you were to travel across Canada from Atlantic to Pacific, you'd discover smaller regional populations with distinctive characters. Atlantic fishing culture with roots in the British Empire, Quebec (a fiercely defensive island of old French colonial culture). Then Ontario and the industries around the

Great Lakes. Toronto and Montreal are both large metropolitan cities filled with Asian, Caribbean, Middle Eastern and European immigrants. Toronto is proud to have one of the most multicultural populations on the planet. And it seems to work very well. Then to the West we have the vast flat and empty prairie lands... cattle, wheat and oil... conservative values... very small towns. And finally the Pacific coast with rich natural resources, very independent liberal minded "hippie" communities contrasted with huge resource industry conservatives... this all closely connected to the US West Coast and the Asia/Pacific rim. The result is that Canadian culture is a sparse and fragile necklace of diverse populations hovering just north of the American cultural machine. Our struggle has been to understand our own cultural diversity (both linguistic and geographic) while resisting US cultural pressures. Our greatest problem is the sparseness of our audience and market place and the ease with which American product can move North and become cheaper competition. And now, Asian business and cultural influences (bolstered by old Commonwealth ties with Hong Kong) are again transforming the Canadian urban experience. I teach in a branch of the University of Toronto where roughly 80 per cent of my students are Asian.

As I've said our population feels cultural pressure from the US. We also feel a vast natural wilderness to the north of us. Toronto is on roughly the same latitude as Rome... Canadian land mass goes clear to the Arctic. In the same latitudes occupied by Europe, (and in a much larger longitudinal land mass) Canada has forests, lakes, rivers.

Two forces influence our search for cultural identity. Powerhouse Empire to the south... Sublime wilderness to the North.... Canadians maintain connections with each other via long stretches of highway... a railroad and a radio network... Closest big cities are often a long day's drive apart. Imagine this and consider the problems of book distribution.

What was the impulse to found 'image nation'? Where did it come from? Who was involved?

We were a bunch of left leaning hippies, poets and artists. To think our effort was entirely conscious would be a mistake. I think that true artists are simply those members of a very small human population who simply have no other choice. We simply found ourselves scratching the same itch together.... and it was gloriously productive. We had a printing press and printed 50 titles a year as well as posters, fine prints and a flood of ephemera. Great artists passed through.

Was it government supported?

'image nation' was supported in part by grants and in part by our own passionate ignorance about the value of our own labour. We worked for free mostly and never thought twice about it. The book was the important thing.

Presumably in return for funding, the state and region asked you to keep 'image nation' "Canadian". Did this compromise your claim to be a cultural publication?

If there was pressure to stay Canadian, I didn't mind it.... didn't call it pressure... saw it as an exuberant celebration of Canadian liberalism. I loved every moment of it... it was so refreshing after the redneck values of pro-war, anti-hippie, America. It just seemed smarter and there was really a lot of material to choose from. As the 1970s evolved, arts groups like the Western Front and General Idea began to promote the concept of a borderless international culture. I was always surprised by how much young Canadians travelled abroad... and this was in stark contract to my more myopic American friends. I actually felt that Canadian artists were very willing to embrace multiculturalism and international cultural networks. If there was a thread of Canadian nationalism in it all, I saw it as a modest defence against American mass media. I still feel that way, although I now see that nationalist habits may have also spawned a mild isolationism. We are not very good at trumpeting our successes to the US, Europe and Pacific Rim. The internet will change that but it may take another generation.

Describe the peer group that contributed to/read the magazine? Was there an associated academic community for instance? Was there support among private galleries?

We were a loose community of artists... we became a stronger community of artists through mutual support and publication. There was nothing formal about it.

Do you remember seeing the National Film Board of Canada production, 'Image'? Was it influential? Any other home-grown magazines that made an impact on photographers?

Yes we knew 'Image'... and it was respected but it was a direct publication of the National Film Board. We were more interested in our non-bureaucratic efforts. There were many literary magazines published through the Coach House Press and some of these had visual components. But there were also other government grant-supported publications by visual artists in Toronto. I felt much closer to these. 'Impulse', 'Impressions', 'FILE', 'photocommuniqué'.

Which critical/artistic currents informed your tenure?

Nothing that academic. But there was a strong neo-Dada current in Canadian culture then. We were close to a group of artists in Vancouver called The Western Front (they still thrive)... and they were connected with Fluxus... and a larger international network of artists.

'image nation' seems to have been heedless of the sorts of debates that polarised the photography sector in the UK at the time (i.e. "documentary" versus "constructed"; black and white versus colour; conceptual versus "art" and so on). Does that ring true? And if so what does that infer that the constituency was pluralistic/tolerant?

I have never believed in one photography... rather I experience a multiplicity of photographies... each a dialect of a larger language. No photograph is really "truthful"... all are editorial opinions. The degree of construction may vary... and the degree to which construction is self evident will change from one photo to another. But every photograph is made during a similar momentary impulse to record some visual sensation with hopes that it will become a visual message. Ansel Adams, Garry Winogrand and Cindy Sherman all choose to twitch their shutter finger exactly when the contents of the frame pleased their political and aesthetic agendas. I have shot both ways myself. I love them both. I once spent five years making frequent trips to Communist Europe. I made 8,000 Hasslebald negatives, each at roughly 1/125 of a second. All together my work represents about 90 seconds worth of random moments in the life of a vast and long-lived population. Out of that series, I have shown perhaps only three or four hundred images. How could this be anything more than a constructed reality? The differences between documentary, constructed, conceptual, fine art, colour, black and white, snapshot, scientific, big format, small format and the like are nothing more that reflections of differences in the personalities of the photographers. I didn't want to live in just one small community of practitioners. Rather I wanted to relish the linguistic differences between one person's photography and another.

The magazine manifested itself in different forms – the "murder research" issue seems so different from the 3-d issue and so on. Can you explain the philosophy, giving examples?

As above... I see many different impulses to the act of making pictures... many resultant differences. Photography is made of impulse and light and exists easily in the many media of the Information Age... television, film, video, slide shows, internet. It is the natural visual language of the Information Age.... quicker than painting and less inherently physical... more naturally ephemeral. [in the 1970s] The Information Age was about to dawn. Artists were gaining access to traditional print media and to video. So we made a magazine that celebrated the diversity of photography.

Was it distributed outside Canada? Where?

Yes and internationally but very sparsely... I was and remain a lousy businessman.

Can you recall the circulation?

We printed between 1000 and 2000 copies of each. Some were distributed well while others hardly made it out of the warehouse. It is truly a rare publication.

Can you remember anything about the editing process?

It changed from issue to issue... sometimes we put out a call... sometimes we found a project ready to go. Sometimes the editing was by ad hoc committee... sometimes I did it solo.

Looking back, how was that era distinct from the present day?

I left the magazine in 1984, just before the personal computer began to become available. Production then was physical, costly and time consuming. Design was difficult to accomplish on a tight budget and good production was beyond our reach. Distribution was also done by hand... inventory control, mailing lists, invoices and accounts were very labour intensive. We could not reach a distribution plateau that could pay good people a good wage. We produced a magazine that sold retail for $6.00 but cost $6.00 to make. We lost money on every wholesale sale. We were gloriously blind to business realities. Today's computers would solve distribution, accounting, design and production problems... ironically, the internet and CD Rom has made paper production less necessary. I still dream of real books for real libraries (Do you know anyone to publish my "Communist Store Window" series?)... but I realize that physical production and distribution is still driven by market tastes... and the more strange a book is, the fewer people there are who want to taste it. So we remain a small band of eccentric artists working on the edge.

You said you were all lefty artist types – were there politics in culture? The war for instance.

The Baby Boom was a political phenomenon in itself. We were bad, sexy and rebellious and there were a lot of us. The political Right was small minded... we were psychedelic. Everything was political... We did change the world but it has been a collective enterprise filled with contradiction. The dance is not over.

How did you end your association with 'image nation'?

I was also working as a holographer, painter and performance artist at the time. All under funded. I got scared once when a major sponsor almost reneged on a promise to cover our printing bills. My holography partner wanted me to focus more attention in the lab. (I left that practice shortly after, as well). It was time to change. I began to travel and write. It felt like the right move to more personal freedom. Then I had a child. So it goes.

Summer 1977

THE DUMB OX

A QUARTERLY ART JOURNAL

5

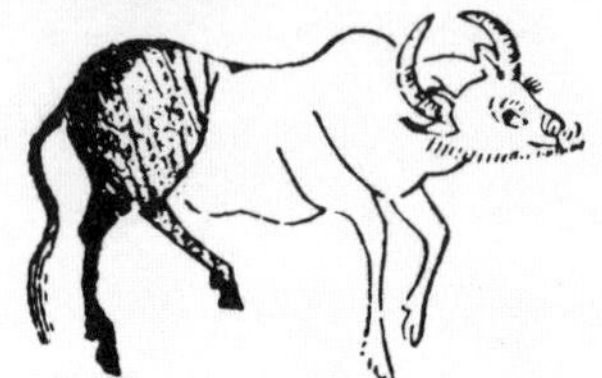

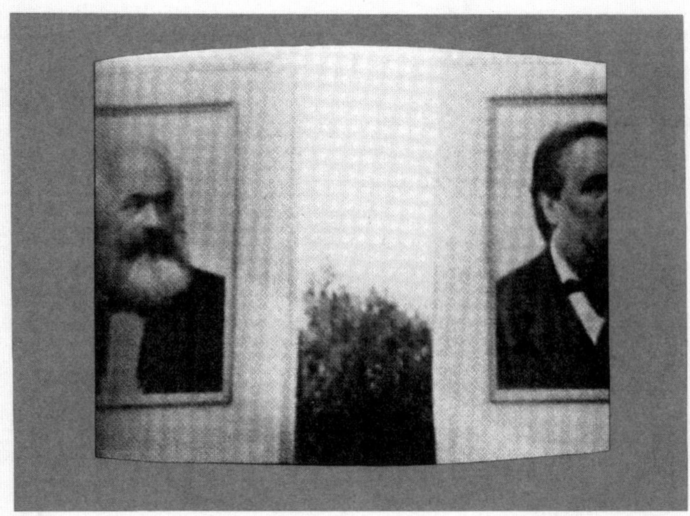

PHOTOGRAPHY AND IDEOLOGY

$1.50

James Hugunin: *The Dumb Ox*

The Los Angeles magazine 'The Dumb Ox' was founded by James Hugunin and Theron Kelley in 1976. The title embraced the latest European theory to provide a lively critique of the institutions of art photography. It folded in 1980.

David Brittain: Can you recreate the cultural scene (locally but also in a broad sense, encompassing photography, art, theory and so on) around the time you were conceiving 'The Dumb Ox'. What task did you want the title to fulfil?

James Hugunin: In 1974 Theron Kelley, who was to become my invaluable co-editor/co-founder of 'The Dumb Ox', was involved with a short-lived Los Angeles art journal, 'Straight Turkey'. It was my exposure to this publishing venture, that brought together art and social concern, that sparked the idea for Theron and I to start our own quarterly journal two years later. We were idealistic "young turks" who were committed to challenging the tenets of formalism/modernism and championing what was to later be known as postmodernism (although this term was not known to us then).

The magazine's title? Theron was very much interested in Oriental philosophy/art and I in Western thought, so the title "The Dumb Ox" was a reference to St. Thomas Aquinas's nickname (and a book by that title on Aquinas by G. K. Chesterton) while the magazine's logo of a prancing ox was taken from a series of Zen drawings on ox-taming (as in referring to taming one's bestial nature). We also loved the title of the literary journal, 'The Unmuzzled Ox', and enjoyed the intertextual connection. Simply put: the title and logo brought together Western rationalism with Eastern mysticism.

The context of the birth of our publication in 1976 was: we both had just finished graduate school, were very dissatisfied with the Los Angeles art/photography scene and wanted to put forth an alternative critical voice that would also provide exposure for many artists we felt were being marginalized (especially conceptually-oriented artists) by the art establishment in LA. The founding of the magazine coincided with my increasing interest in doing art criticism and it was my earliest venue for my writings. Exposure of my writing therein opened doors to other publications. Theoretically, the magazine had much in common with Lew Thomas's Photography and Language movement in the San Francisco Bay area at the time (Lew guest edited one of our issues). The Los Angeles art photography scene was dominated by Robert Heinecken's photo-sculpture and manipulated imagery (he was my grad mentor at UCLA) and so the scene had an aversion to the kind of conceptual-based photo-language practice that I was involved in; my artwork, writing, and new quarterly journal were more favourably received by Northern Californians rather than Southern. Due to this affinity with

Northern California, many thought our magazine was published out of the Bay area. Very quickly, however, our journal caught on in Los Angeles and grew to have international subscribers.

Was the photo scene in LA in 1976 divided between the modernists and the rest? Was Aperture the bible? I am trying to get more of a sense of the scene and what The Dumb Ox saw itself as opposed to.

The LA photo scene was dominated by alternative processes (cyanotype, gum bichromate, etc.) and photo sculpture and was largely hostile to mixing art and politics; this influence was much less in the SF Bay area where Lew Thomas was a prominent figure in promoting a structuralist/textualist model of photography which touched on problems of how we come to know and act in the world. The LA scene was quite hostile to an intellectual approach to the medium and the intrusion of a language model into analysis and practice of art photography. At the time, I was reading Marx, Husserl, Merleau-Ponty, Wittgenstein, Ayer, Barthes, Foucault. I was very interested in knowledge theory and focused on that in my philosophy studies. Theories and practice of Minimalism and Post-Minimalism were important to me in terms of the issue they raised for epistemology, as were Allan Kaprow's work and writings (like 'The Education of the Un-Artist'). Afterimage was an important publication for me and later the quarterly journal October.

I also consistently read 'Critical Inquiry', adapting the debates therein (mostly on literature) to photography. I was being influenced by postmodern literature too, even more so than looking at photographs. I can't recall 'Aperture' being much of an influence on me (except the earlier issues edited by Minor White whom I saw as a proto-postmodernist for his interest in language and the problems of interpretation, i.e., reading a photograph).

According to myth the LA photo scene, when compared with the East Coast scene, was hedonistic and open to hybrid ways of operating. This may betray the fact that photo history – as far as I can see – was written by East Coast people. I wonder if you thought of 'The Dumb Ox' as a West Coast (as well as a post-modern) voice? And how compatible West Coast-post-modern were at the time.

Yes, despite my outsider status in the LA photo scene (i.e., being more appreciated in the San Francisco Bay area) I did see 'The Dumb Ox' as a West Coast publication devoted to a strong opposition to the East Coast Szarkowskian formalist approach. Once when Peter Galassi came to UCLA to lecture on his and Szarkowski's 'Before Photography' exhibition, us editors sat in the front row and harangued him with questions. When we also showed up at his lecture at USC the following day, he saw us and cut short his question-answer period to avoid dealing with us. What did unite Southern California photo scene with its Northern counterpart was a strong dislike of the narrow Greenbergian style definition Szarkowski had of what constituted legitimate photographic practice.

I am sorry to say that I don't know the photography and language movement. Can you give me a quick introduction from the standpoint of its influence on you?

'Photography and Language' (a book and an exhibition at what was then La Mamelle Gallery run by Carl Loeffler and now is Camera Work Gallery) was largely inspired by Lew Thomas and his NSF Press publications (like 'Structuralism and Photography', 'Photography the Problematic Model', 'Photography and Eroticism'). The gist was to see photographic practice through the lens of Barthesian structuralism, i.e., the photo as text and how text might interact with photographic imagery ("anchor" and "relay" in Barthes' terminology).

Influences on my approach to photography goes back to 1968 when a friend sent me a copy of 'Aspen' magazine, an issue devoted conceptual art (featuring Ed Ruscha's 'Thirty-Four Parking Lots' and other conceptual uses of photography). I later studied under Jerry McMillan at California State University, Northridge who was a childhood buddy of Ruscha's (we toured Ed's studio once) and championed challenging all assumptions about photographic practice. Heinecken's work also was appealing to me for its challenge to the Szarkowskian model.

'The Dumb Ox' was a product of those passions and might be gathered together with other seventies publications and articles (Coleman's 'Village Voice' columns for instance) that constitute what came in advance of 'October'. Do you see any affinities with anyone else at that time. 'Afterimage' (I suppose).

Yes, I saw 'The Dumb Ox' as having affinities with 'Afterimage'; in fact, I started writing for that publication soon after 'The Dumb Ox' caught the editorial staff's attention.

Also the tone of 'The Dumb Ox' was very carefully pitched – angry perhaps but always humorous. How did that come about?

I think the humour in our publication came from a shared sense of humour between Theron and I and a commitment to humour as social weapon (I still teach an Art and Humour class and humour is a central element in all my work) and the fact that I never take myself so seriously I can't laugh at myself.

Can you tell me about the nitty-gritty. Why that initial format? And how/why did it change? How did you fund it and how did you get it distributed?

We chose the tabloid format as it was inexpensive (as I worked at a print shop I was able to shoot at stats, hi-con negatives and halftones for free); later we chose the book format for the artists books issue (issue #4); everyone loved the new format, so we kept it, having Barry Singer (a Cal Arts MFA grad and fellow artist) owner of Singer Printing do the press work (but I would often help burn plates, clean the press, etc. at his shop to cut costs of production).

We distributed the mag ourselves around Los Angeles book stores which took 'The Dumb Ox' on consignment. In addition, we mailed copies to major book outlets around the country and overseas. EBSCO [subscription agency] was used for subscriptions. At our peak we had over 400 yearly paid subscribers and a press run of 1500 copies. We once even got a letter from some obscure place in India asking for a free subscription (which we gladly gave, as we also gave out free subscriptions to prison inmates – we had several passionate inmate subscribers who loved the mag.).

Do you know if your readers were photography people? I am guessing here that in the mid seventies those who were into semiotics and who got the jokes about formalism, would be the "artists"; the kind of people you admired and who liked Ruscha. I suppose that begs the question: where did you sell most copies?

I would say our subscribers generally held to a more intellectual, theoretical approach to their work and ideas, regardless of what medium they worked in. LA artists were, in general, less theoretically oriented than those in Northern California. Due to The School of the Art Institute's historical interest in artist's publications, when I came to teach there in 1985, 'The Dumb Ox's' reputation preceded me and I was a minor celebrity when I first arrived. The Flaxman Library there did a retrospective exhibit of all the 'The Dumb Ox' and 'U-Turn' issues. SAIC's Joan Flasch artists' book collection has all my titles (artist books and quarterlies).

What is the relationship between the artist's book and the artist's magazine? To what extent was 'The Dumb Ox' your art? What of the other contributors?

I started doing self-published artist's books very early in my production; it was a way of rejecting the commercialization of art. I wanted to present art that would be affordable and in multiples. However, I wanted to extend my concerns into a broader audience and more toward social issues. I did see 'The Dumb Ox' as a collaborative form of art that traced the lively debates Theron and I would often have about art and society (we extended that dialogue by inviting guest editors to do issues). For instance, the last issue was put together by Allan Kaprow and Paul McCarthy.

In doing 'The Dumb Ox', ultimately I learned an enormous amount from my exchange of ideas with Theron (we all called him "Terry"), Kenon Breazeale (an art historian), and Janice Tieken (an artist) (both came on board at different times to provide editorial input from a woman's perspective) and from the many artists we featured.

Perhaps you can explain how you saw editorial changes happen and what caused these.

After issue #3, we felt we'd laid out our main theoretical focus so we wanted to open the pages to other people with interesting ideas that resonated with our editorial focus.

Did the magazine promote the multiples? And did it promote multiples by other artists?

We didn't promote multiples per se (although the artists' books issue implied that). Had the internet been available back then, we'd have never gone the hard copy route, but would've gone wholly digital so as to reach thousands of potential viewers. We were just twenty years too early.

I see the magazine was short-lived. Was that because it had done its job? How did you fund it anyhow?

Actually 'The Dumb Ox's' last issue was very expensive to produce and we had 500 more copies printed than normal, but we were counting on selling issues like hotcakes at a forthcoming Performance Conference in LA that would prominently feature Kaprow and McCarthy. The original artwork that Kaprow provided from various sources was of poor quality, so the reproductions were not great (no fault of our printer); moreover, Kaprow objected to something in the cover design, but McCarthy had done the cover and had signed off on the proofs. Well, Kaprow went ballistic, refused to allow us to sell our magazine at the conference (if we did he threatened to destroy our reputations!). Kaprow had been a kind of idol of mine and this incident popped that bubble. So the magazine sat idle and we lost a lot of money and the magazine died as all our funds were exhausted (the mag was funded by the editors, no grant monies were ever used). A year later Kaprow apologized to us for being a jerk about it, he said he was going through a divorce and was on edge. But that didn't prevent the magazine from going belly up.

It took two years of recharging my creative batteries to launch a new publication, 'U-Turn', with new editors (Theron was now working in the film industry as an editor and had little time to commit).

I wonder if you could give me some sense of your thinking as you contemplated changing from a magazine that was essentially your soapbox – that you could control – to something of a collaborative situation. That seems like a big move from being in control to being partners.

The purpose of 'The Dumb Ox' was to provide exposure to new ideas and give people a voice that had none at the time, so it was natural to have guest editors. I, of course, still oversaw the reviews section in each issue. This participatory aspect to my work was also reflected in many conceptual pieces of mine which I called "Participations" (the works involved people participating in a structured way to complete the work, here's the Kaprow influence).

October was obviously some high point in the critique of modernist photography. By seventy-six how far do you think that critique had become widespread within magazines?

'The Dumb Ox' came out prior to 'October's' first issue (which we critically reviewed). I recall being interested in Allan Sekula's critical writing, regardless of which publications ran his work. I was more focused on specific authors rather than thinking about a particular mag's orientation toward the issues, so I can't address that point.

Was there a point in the editorial evolution when the anomalous aspects of the modernist discourse began to outlive their usefulness as a catalyst for critical discussion?

I would say that for me, by the 1990s, critical writing on photography came to intrigue me less as the Szarkowskian paradigm lost its hold.

How is the e-zine a better vehicle for ideas than the paper magazine?

The e-zine incarnation of 'U-Turn' is far superior to having to do hard copy version because: 1) small production costs; 2) vast audience reach; 3) ease of production in gathering materials: people can email us files or one can simply hyperlink to various web pages to produce an issue.

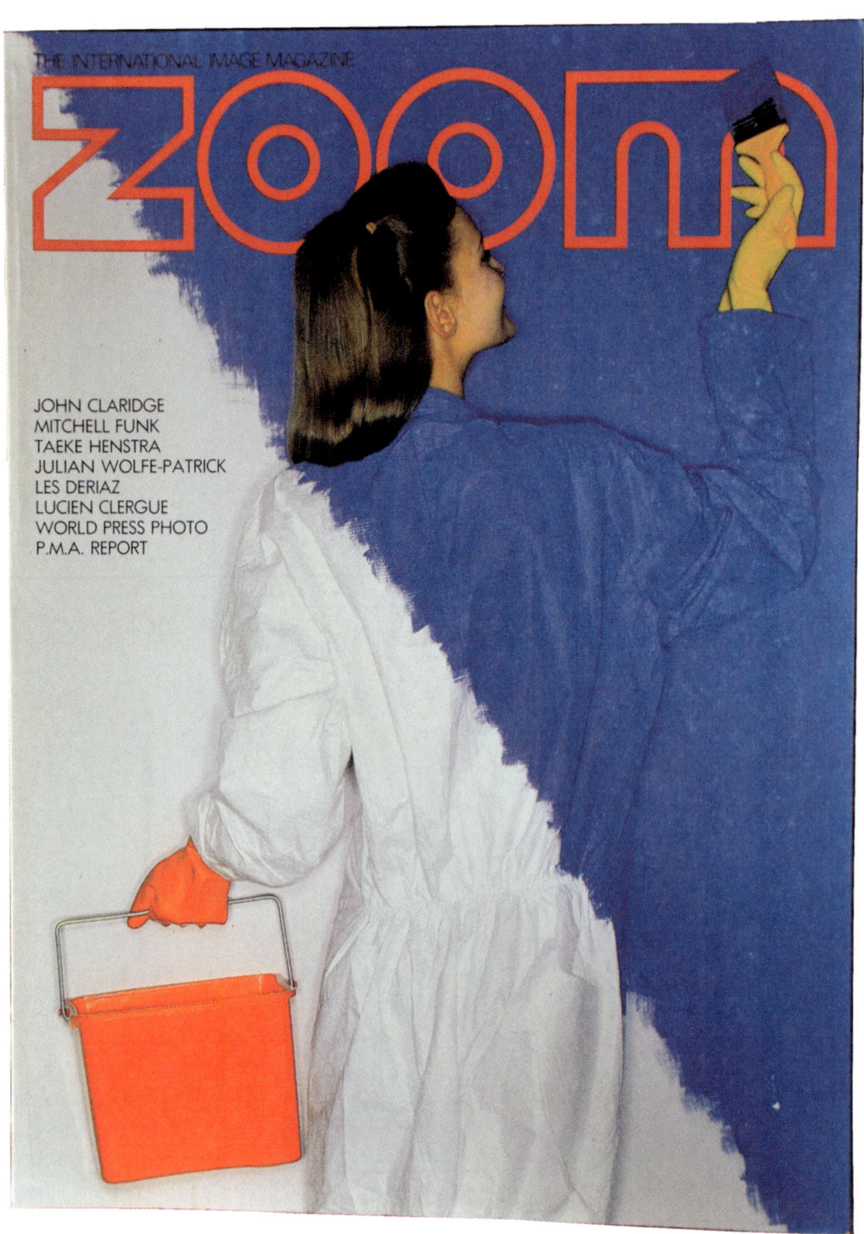
THE INTERNATIONAL IMAGE MAGAZINE
ZOOM
JOHN CLARIDGE
MITCHELL FUNK
TAEKE HENSTRA
JULIAN WOLFE-PATRICK
LES DERIAZ
LUCIEN CLERGUE
WORLD PRESS PHOTO
P.M.A. REPORT

Jack Schofield: *English Zoom*

'Zoom' was founded in Paris by a commercial publisher. In 1978 an English edition appeared and Jack Schofield was its editor for the first ten issues. 'Zoom' was unrivalled among photographic magazines as the only 'glossy' to be generously supported by the trade.

David Brittain: How did you get involved with 'Zoom'?

Jack Schofield: I met Joel Laroche, who was the guy who ran it, in France. I guess he found me because I was editing camera magazines in the UK – 'Photo Technique', at the time. We got on very well and I started doing work for 'Zoom'. I had to fly to Paris – sometimes two or three times a week. When I met him, he was a magazine publisher. I suppose there was a UK equivalent – maybe Felix Dennis might be close. Joel used to do cartoon magazines, poster magazines – he was opportunistic. He started a skateboard magazine when skateboards were fashionable, and I did some work for that. 'Zoom' was clearly the most important thing he did, but he was willing to do anything to turn an honest penny. We both got involved in computing around the same time. He wanted to use computers for illustration. He started a computer graphics magazine, which turned out to be very successful, I think.

Originally 'Zoom' was Paris-based, but Joel had the idea of expanding it globally. The thing about 'Zoom' was the colour – at the time, practically everything was in black and white. Colour was very expensive. We had a very good deal on colour printing from a company called Istra in Strasbourg, who were mainly known for printing knitting patterns. To them, 'Zoom' was a kind of flagship "look what we can do" kind of product. They were wonderful. I used to go to Istra to see 'Zoom' off the press, and I had huge admiration for the guys there. They would always go the extra mile, and they would always want to do it better than you did.

The basic idea was that 'Zoom' had limited circulation in France and limited potential elsewhere, but you could do five-colour printing – four colours and black. So, basically Joel went around Europe and invited other publishers to launch editions of 'Zoom' using the same colour plates, because that would make it affordable. So we would print up to five languages in two days. All the colour was done the same, and you just changed the black plate. So you'd have a French run with French black (text plate), then you'd take the French black off and you'd put the English black on, to get a longer run.

Black was text. So it was the same pictures for everyone?

It was the same pictures everywhere, but they weren't always in the same order. We used to work in sections of 16 or 32 pages, so you could drop a section. Typically, I would say: I will take that French section and that

French section, but in between I'm going to have an English section. Or, I could do a section that the French would take. So, for instance, I did a feature on Hipgnosis [the company that designed many of the Pink Floyd album covers], and their album covers at that time, and the French did their translation of my Hipgnosis article. The idea was that everybody would be able to contribute if they had good stuff. The opening section with the contents and gallery listings would be all in English because this would never be in any other edition.

Was there a central place where all the material was pooled?

Paris.

In Paris the editors of the Italian and other issues decided what was going to be in their issues?

No, we worked independently; people just decided which French sections they wanted. The French printed every month, so you would have to sometimes stockpile pages. If you came out four or five times a year then you could have stuff sitting around for a month or two before you'd get it into an issue. That's why we didn't put page numbers on the colour sections.

How could the French sustain 'Zoom' as a monthly?

It was very, very popular. The French had more taste. The French magazine Photo was really successful, and they had some great reportage magazines.

You worked for a London-based publisher?

Yes. I worked for Penblade Publishers, where at various times I edited 'Photo Technique', 'Film Making' and the 'Royal Photographic Society's Journal', and we did a magazine for the British Institute of Professional Photographers. So it was a small publisher that concentrated on photographic magazines. Obviously, there's not a big market for doing a magazine for the Royal Photographic Society but, of course, the key benefit was efficiency. You're talking to the same advertisers, so there're fewer overheads in selling adverts – not that there was very much advertising in 'Zoom'.

The French 'Zoom' was very successful and Joel believed that it could be very successful in other places. To his enormous credit, Penblade's publisher, Terry Griffiths, backed that idea and launched it in the UK. We had a do at Langan's Brasserie, and Adrian Flowers made a nice little speech.

So how did it sell in the UK?

It turned out the UK market was not worth it! But for Joel, a big reason for doing the UK edition was to create English language content that could be repackaged for the American edition. I am not privy to the figures on that. But the UK print run started out at 15,000 and if we sold ten we were pretty lucky. We had about 2500 subscriptions. 'Zoom' was £2.50, which was a lot of money then – four times the cost an average magazine. But it was hard to compete. One of the bookstores at Heathrow took us off the shelves – it was one of our biggest outlets, selling a couple of hundred a month. They said, "Well, it's revenue per foot. If we put 'Cosmopolitan' there we'd sell thousands."

Ten thousand isn't bad...

This was intended to be a popular magazine. We tried really hard to interest people who weren't terribly interested in photography but were interested in graphics and images and being chic. The "book" had two main functions: one of them was to publish really good photography that no one had seen before. If you look at the first issue, from 1979, I honestly believe you could put that on the bookstalls today and it wouldn't look out of date. At the time, it was really fresh.

Joel and I – famously – once got into a car and drove around California and, you know, we'd ring up, for instance, Ansel Adams and say, "We're in California – can we come round and see you?" And he'd say "Yes" or "No" (he said yes). We went round to the local photo galleries to see if there was somebody we'd never heard of (we wanted people nobody here had heard of) who was really good, and we used to drive round there and interview them. You never got any money but you got 10 or 20 copies of the magazine per page, I think. So if you had 16 pages you got a whole lot of copies.

You see, if you sent someone like John Thornton [the advertising photographer] enough copies, they would give them to all their friends – and a lot of their friends would be top art directors. So you were providing a display case for photographers to reach art directors with ideas that maybe they couldn't do commercially. We would get photographers ringing up saying: "I'd like to do you a cover". They'd spend a fortune doing a cover specifically for 'Zoom' because it enabled them to do an idea that they really wanted to do. It was advertising for them. It was free advertising, in a sense.

With 'Photo Technique' the focus was very clear: you had a reader who had a camera and he didn't know what to do; he fancied taking photographs but he didn't know what to take photographs of. And your huge victory was when some housewife sent you a wonderful picture of a red pepper against a black background, improvised from a garbage bag, and it was really sharp. You felt that you had achieved something because you had helped someone to do something that was creative and interesting ... But 'Zoom' was very different. (Ha! Ha!) Because you weren't trying to do that.

You might have several different things in mind. "This guy is a wonderful, famous photographer so you've got to buy this issue." Famous within their own area, perhaps, like Irena Ionescu. Then you've got these other people, the ones we tried to find, that nobody had heard of – or maybe had only been seen in an art gallery in California or South Africa or Japan. We did a lot of Japanese. Not just photography but graphics, adverts, historical images.

Who was your reader?

My target reader was professional photographers, advertising agencies, media buyers – the business, students, sophisticated amateurs. People interested in images. Because you couldn't compete with AP ('Amateur Photographer'). The volume of 'Zoom', the separations, the costs of printing: you would need a lot of advertising to support 100,000 copies. It wasn't there.

What was the 'Zoom' idea of a "good picture"?

There wasn't an idea of a good picture – that was what made 'Zoom' great. We used to have these arguments about whether something was good or not – but actually we didn't really care. We appreciated craft: there was something that came with being really, really well crafted, so that was a good reason for publishing something. Then there was famous photography and portfolios you got from new books. Then there was stuff that was, well, had anyone seen it before? The great thing about 'Zoom' was the willingness to publish things – even if we were a bit doubtful about them – on the grounds that this guy had something to say and he really wanted to say it.

There was sense in which 'Zoom' provided raw material and ideas for art directors and other photographers. There was never any sense that you were trying to find the 50 greatest black and white pictures of all time – that this was immortal. You were trying to say: "Who's doing what now, and why are they doing it? What's interesting?" Joel was always looking for things that were "very fun".

Some editors felt that they instinctively knew the best work – but unlike you they felt they were on a mission.

We didn't know what the best work was. We had the this-is-going-to-be-wonderful-for-fifteen-minutes attitude. We wanted to have an impact and knock your eyes out, but if you go back a year later, as I have done, maybe you see whether you were right to run something, with hindsight. There was no attempt to canonize things. It was a "pick and mix" kind of operation.

That sense of discovery must have been exhilarating. The 'Creative Camera' of this period reflects the same excitement – because so much material was being uncovered.

We didn't see 'Creative Camera' as being commercial, while a lot of our stuff was commercial. Our contributors were mostly professional photographers, so they were doing it for money. Christian Vogt, for example, you might say he is a commercial art photographer. Sometimes they were commercial photographers who were doing something interesting on the side.

The contents are a tremendous clash of advertising, reportage, historical art photography. I suppose it was meant to be an index of what was out there then.

Yes, there wasn't any set plan. Some of it was great photography and some of it was crap, but it didn't matter. It reflected what was going on. If you did a "Zoom goes to California" issue – if it was happening in California, it could go in. It didn't have to meet any golden rules. It had to be at least interesting for the 15 minutes that you might see it.

Zoom was famous for its sub-porn. Was there a policy there? At 'Amateur Photographer' there was a golden rule about putting what was called "glamour" on every cover.

No, we didn't.

What, no discussion about the impact of glamour on sales?

No. We were more or less impervious to it. Obviously, we had some of it because a lot of the interesting stuff that was happening was happening in that world. I don't honestly think you can say Christian Vogt is sub-porn.

The view was that 'Zoom' was titillating.

I would say that if we'd thought it was porn we wouldn't have published it – unless it was, say, historical porn or whatever. We might well do something that was erotic, but we didn't go out looking for erotic pictures. We'd go out looking for things that were different. If they happened to be erotic then that might be a nice bonus. We were never against eroticism!

How did the illustration fit it?

'Zoom' was an image magazine, not a photography magazine – it says on the front: "the image magazine". So we had discussions where we might have said, "What illustration can we get?" because, clearly there was a danger of photography overruning the whole thing. Which you didn't want. You wanted to have record covers and adverts and stuff that was designed. It was an essential part of the agenda: not to be a camera magazine. We were trying to benefit from the photo magazine market and sell to it without that being a limitation. We wanted to be on trendy people's coffee tables.

You could always open 'Zoom' and find something really interesting – even if most of it didn't appeal.

Yes! That was success. If you were on an art director's budget then you were probably buying it on expenses, and you'd pay two quid for one picture. And cheap at the price.

Was it more like a catalogue than a magazine?

Yes, absolutely.

Would you say 'Zoom' was in the business of supporting photography?

Yes. Promoting photography, promoting originality and art... If you forget that a picture started as a double-page ad selling cornflakes or whatever – if you take it out of that context and you reproduce it really beautifully and give it (say it's by Marty Evans) the kind of respect that you would give an art photograph, or a photograph by Cartier-Bresson, you can look at it purely as an image. If it's done really well, it's worthy of respect. It may give you an idea.

If you have done – as I have – successful magazines then you know how this kind of thing works. You have the letters pages, the news page, the book reviews, the columns, the departments and all that, so in an average magazine you could have 40 pages of routine stuff and only 6 or 8 pages of stuff that was new and exciting, like portfolios. 'Zoom' was the reverse. We would have 100 pages of portfolios and 5 or 6 pages of this other stuff.

I liked Andy Warhol's 'Interview' magazie. I liked the generosity of it. The trouble with most commercial magazines is – increasingly – if you want someone to read something, you put 50 words in a box, and there are hundreds of things happening on the page. The great thing about 'Zoom', 'Rolling Stone' and a few others was the sense of "Let's make it big." 'Nova', of course, was another one. It had the idea that if you picked it up it wouldn't necessarily be predictable.

A lot of readers want their publication to slide on like a warm sock – you always know where the crossword is and where the editorial is, so there's a lot of habit forming, reassurance and satisfaction. It works. If you want to do a successful magazine, that's what you do. Never move stuff around. You give the reader a home from home that's comfortable, where they know where things are, and the things that are there are satisfying. People remember that 'Nova' once gave away a wall poster that asked readers to take the magazine apart and stick the bits together. Well, fantastic! But there's a reaction against that. Nova at its best had the ability to throw away the flight plan and do X Y or Z.

You have to be really committed to do things like this. When you're running a magazine, you hire a guy to write a column, and it falls in the door and you don't have to think about it. So a large proportion of a magazine just runs itself. You can go away for two weeks, have a holiday, and when you come back, you know, the machinery works. That's quite different from deciding to do a whole issue about Polaroid, or California, or Japan, because then you have to start from scratch. There's obviously much more work involved.

So 'Zoom' promoted photography, yet wasn't a photography magazine. Was there something in this format that was unique. Was there anything like it?

There was 'The Image' magazine, produced by David Bailey and David Litchfield. That was the thing I saw in the UK market that was a kind of wake-up call.

How did you see what you did in relation to the "world" of photography such as it was then; galleries?

One thing I tried not to have too much of was, what you might call realistic photography. I didn't go for the reportage: I always wanted things that didn't look like real life. I always wanted things in which the image sort of transcended the reportorial aspect.

Yes, so the word image is important then?

Yes.

Did the word image then mean what it does now; you know both an image and your image?

Yes. Absolutely. There was a lot of exasperation that 'Zoom' was elitist. But it was elitism in a democratic way – because you could join the elite just by buying the magazine.

My sense was that if you were a buyer you might like a third of it. The thing was, somebody else might like a different third and somebody else a different third. It seems to me that if you gave them one or two portfolios that they really loved then you could satisfy that reader, even if they didn't like the rest. What I didn't want was a magazine that would satisfy him a hundred per cent, because if you did that, you would have something that was very narrow. Of course, if you're after the art director market, they're butterflies. It's a fashion business. In a sense, 'Zoom' was a fashion magazine for people in advertising and design.

You're trying to pick up what's new, like a jackdaw. You have a number of feeders. The Photographers' Gallery was clearly one. And books. You might be able to get 16 pages from a book, and you might even get the colour separations, which were very expensive at the time. Degree shows – there was some good stuff from degree shows. You plundered other magazines – Avenue from Holland, 'Vogue', anything from Japan – these were the places you would look for stuff. If you go for people who are masters of their craft, you can usually leave the art bit up to them.

So you're saying that there were two strands to your editing: one was non-judgemental, eclectic, and the other was being sure that the photography was at least interesting, but it couldn't be "realistic". You must have been pulling out a lot of black and white documentary stuff – that was the heyday of it.

Yes. That wasn't our bag. We did some UK-based people, such as Ian Berry, but the French did much more reportage. The German version of 'Zoom' was really very sexy. It had a lot of high quality – not quite porn… They spent much more money than we did. What went for 'Zoom' in the UK and the US didn't necessarily go for the Germans, or vice versa.

There was a kind of permanence about 'Zoom', wasn't there? You could pin up the pictures from it. I bet they never had an art magazine that allowed people to do that. Have you ever thought what the relationship is between the reproduction and the photograph?

The thing about a photograph on a page is that it can be almost as good as or maybe better than a print, partly through context and partly through the quality of the reproduction. You can actually have something that is really close to the real thing. If you ever go to an exhibition of an artist such as [George] Rouault, who puts paint on an inch thick, you can't possibly reproduce that. You lose almost everything.

Most of the contributors to 'Zoom' were shooting for the page. At the time a gallery was a rarity.

Practically everybody that we used was shooting for the page, or for the album cover – Hipgnosis did a book of their covers, so in a sense that was for the page, too.

This alternative position you're referring to: the 'Creative Camera' and 'Ten.8' people saw themselves as a bit left field and outside commercial publishing. Was Zoom your opportunity to be anti-commercial publishing?

No, I don't think so. We were very closely aligned with the commercial publishing industry. We loved art directors, we loved photographers, we loved galleries, we loved book publishers. At the same time we were looking for things that you couldn't show anywhere else. We never felt we were anti-commercial or non-commercial. We wanted to sell magazines; we never wanted to change the world in any real sense. We wanted to make it prettier – more interesting, really. Why have really boring ads when you can have nice ads?

Obviously there was no discussion about taking any critical perspective to bear on any of it.

The reader had to do his own critique. What was interesting was that it was really very hard to decide what was very good. Even from your own point of view as a consumer of what you're producing, it wasn't always clear what was good and what was bad. But it did come out of commercial milieu – or a milieu that could be commercialised, that had a wider resonance.

Were all these source books like 'Black Book' around at the time?

Yes, we used to go through source books looking for stuff and then contact the photographers.

As you say, this is not a photography magazine – but about images. But it brings stuff into its remit that you don't think of as image – I mean Lartigue's autochromes, for instance. They seem closer to painting. For you reportage wasn't image but it was for the French. What then is meant by the word image?

For me, if you said "image" you were in some sense divorcing it from reality. You were looking at it as an object, as a self-contained thing, and to some extent separate from what it referred to in the real world. There was an abstraction involved. When you said, "this is an image," you were saying that it may have been a photograph of this scene at that time, but nevertheless – in this context – you could look at it as if it wasn't. You could look at it as a self-referential image, as a work of art – how is it composed, and all of that stuff. It's not necessarily comfortable to do that with reportage.

Was 'Zoom' interested in art?

We weren't an art magazine: we much preferred commercial artists. So you might take commercial illustration and look at it as if it was art. Stuff that was art to begin with was less interesting, because you already knew how to look at it. With hindsight, perhaps it was a sort of Pop-art thing –

people like Peter Blake and Roy Lichtenstein were also playing with the interface between context and content.

You weren't averse to publishing Weston or Adams – which was, at the time, art?

Yes. We had to do some familiar stuff because people will buy a magazine if it's got a name that they recognise, and in a sense, the presence of some famous well-crafted work vouches for the rest. But we didn't want to go down the portfolio route that, at the time, would have been to base the magazine on Bailey, Lategan, Ansel Adams, Cartier-Bresson, all the big names. But all of that stuff you could already see in bookshops or in other magazines. That was a good reason for us not to do it. The idea with 'Zoom' was not to have the pictures everybody else had. Why would you buy the magazine? You could get a beautiful Bill Brandt book instead.

I couldn't remember how much of that photography archive was widely availaible.

Aperture books was doing a lot of stuff. There was a fairly healthy book market. There was 'Camera', the Swiss magazine. It was a beautiful magazine but it seemed very sterile – altogether far too clean. It was closer to 'Zoom' in many respects than anything else. It had the ability to run things at length. The ability to show things that people weren't generally publishing. Very nice display – in a sense, better display than 'Zoom'. It was much more of an art gallery type of magazine.

You mean the white space?

Yes. It treasured work more. We wanted to present stuff beautifully, no doubt about that, but we didn't want to do it in an art gallery style, in a slightly precious way. Camera was a bit like a miniature book – the presentation was book-like or gallery-like, whereas we were much more into magazines. With magazines, there's a great throwaway aspect – it's part of the magazine culture. Although we were definitely not trying to be thrown away, we did have a much more throwaway attitude.

There is something of the business about 'Zoom' – that you had to be in the image biz to read it.

Yes, but like I said, you could join in for two quid. You could pick up a copy of 'Geo' or 'Vogue' or something like that and find great photography in it – but it's not there because it's great photography. They have another agenda. You could find photographers in these magazines that you could take out of there and put into another context where you would look at them in a different way. So in a sense we were doing a job for readers by consuming a lot of magazines and importing the best pictures into different contexts.

What was the photographers' sense of the context of 'Zoom'? Did they think it was an art context?

I think they felt recognised. We never tried to set a standard or to say, "this is good enough and this isn't good enough". There was never the kind of quality barrier that 'Swiss Camera' had. We took the line: is it different? Is it interesting? If it was transitory, it didn't matter. Is it transitory? Great! There was a sense of amusement about it. You would never try to be worthy. 'Swiss Camera' did have a good mixture of material, but there was something very worthy about it. I'm not knocking it: it was just different.

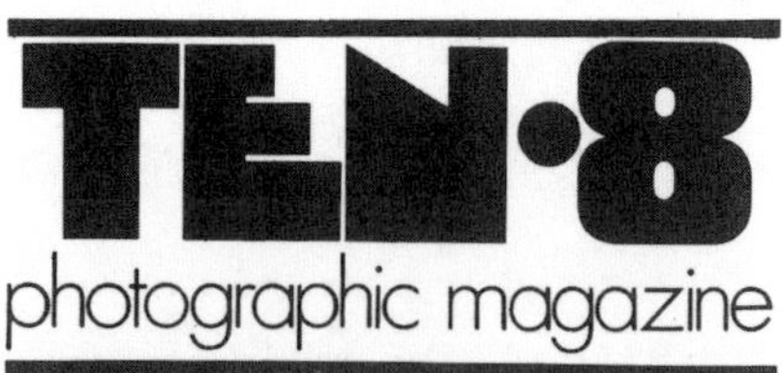

NUMBER 1 FEBRUARY 1979. 50p.

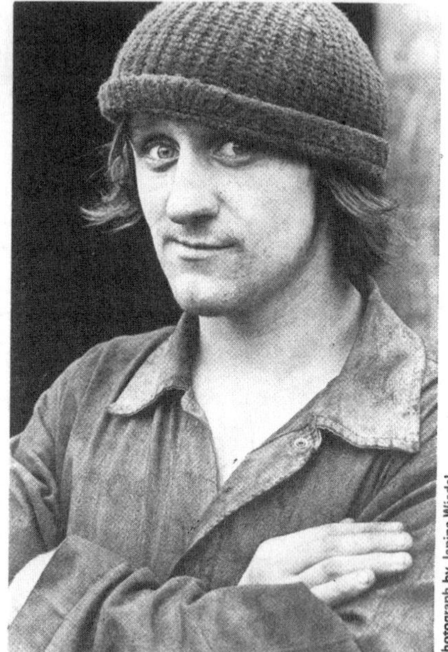

Photograph by Janine Wiedel

FIRST ISSUE:

Work by Janine Wiedel, Rob Moore, John Myers
The growth of Community Photography
How 'real' is Social Documentary?
plus News

Derek Bishton: *Ten.8*

'Ten.8' was co-founded in Birmingham, England in 1979 by Derek Bishton, Brian Homer and John Reardon. It began as a platform for the city's photographers but soon developed an issue-based focus and was distributed internationally until it folded in 1994. A former journalist, Bishton worked with a shifting cast of editors that included David A. Bailey, John Taylor and Rhonda Wilson, among others.

David Brittain: What were the origins of Ten.8?

Derek Bishton: The origins are pretty parochial. In the late seventies I was working with Brian Homer and John Reardon. Brian Homer is still based in Birmingham; he is better known as a graphic designer. I worked on newspapers and left newspapers. I worked at Birmingham Arts Lab, did various alternative things. I came together with Brian because we could see that in the inner city of Birmingham there was a lot going on and there was a huge need for people who had design and journalistic skills. There was so much stuff being produced then; the seventies was the great crucible for a lot of inner city issues. Clare Short was running a project just round the corner. Because I was a journalist I ended up editing lots of things people wanted to produce. Brian and I could see there was quite a reasonable alternative career to be made producing these things, so we set up a little design studio and the first thing we did was a book about Rastafarians which Clare Short had commissioned because there was a huge issue about black kids on the street: you know, what's it all about? That kind of stuff. So we were doing a lot of that kind of work, I had just personally become interested in photography; almost as a sideline to all the work we were doing. I said to Brian, "What Birmingham really needs is a gallery. Because there's nowhere people can focus their attention on photography." I had a Camerawork model [the photography organisation in East London] in mind I suppose.

At that point did you have contact with 'Camerawork'?

Not intimate contact, but we did through the Birmingham members – like Nick Hedges and Ed Barber, although Ed wasn't a Brummy. Ed and Jenny Matthews were part of that core group of people who were involved with 'Camerawork' over the years – Chris Steele-Perkins was too, just before he joined the Magnum photo agency. So we had some contacts with people who'd been involved with it and it seemed like it was the right kind of model for it was an activist organisation and it was photo-led. The interesting thing about all these people was that they were very good photographers – even though politics was, as it were, on top of the agenda.

You had seen their magazine?

Yeah. It was that that inspired us.

What was it like then?

You know the early editions of 'Ten.8' that opened up? It was like that. We nicked everything from them in terms of concept, idea; not necessarily the politics – although of course the politics of 'Ten.8' were leftish. At that stage I was more interested in asking where was Birmingham's photographic community, rather that what can this photographic community do …

Was that a big difference between your organisation and 'Camerawork'?

Yeah. We just didn't know anyone.

'Camerawork' wasn't interested in promoting photography as art either.

They weren't at that stage. But when you look at the subsequent work of the key members of that group, you realise that deep down, yes they were. At that point issues like Northern Ireland, racism, issues about black people in the inner city were all very close to what we were experiencing in Birmingham. There seemed to be a lot of parallels then. It was just such a sexy product at the time. It opened out, it had big pages fabulous big photographs occasionally. And I said to Brian, "What we need to do is produce something like this and we can get something going up here." So we made an application to West Midlands Arts; we said we want to start a photography magazine (they were pole-axed). Who are these strange people who are asking to produce a photography magazine? I am trying to think who was the photography officer then… Anyway, they came out to see us, realised that we actually had the technical skills to do a magazine (because we had been producing books, magazines, leaflets) and agreed – as long as we took on board some people West Midlands Arts considered to be responsible, OK people.

They wanted a board?

Yeah. The usual bollocks. As it turned out almost all of them were really good people. They included Nick Hedges, John Taylor and couple of others who were important at the early stage but didn't actually play a huge role after the first couple of years. So a group of people came together – mainly based around Stourbridge College of Art, which had a very vibrant photography course at that time. John was teaching there, Nick Hedges was there; a guy called Rob Moore was there who made a lot of large format photography. I was completely self-taught as a photographer; I had never studied it. Brian was the same as me; he had worked for the Central Electricity Generating Company and had dropped out, to become a prime mover in Birmingham's alternative newspapers at that time – 'Time Out' type magazines. So we had a good record of publishing and an ability to produce stuff. We just didn't have very much of a handle on photography, other than just a general interest as people who were beginning to grapple with some of the issues about stereotyping, you know: how a white person moves in a largely mixed culture, power relations. All of those issues were beginning to surface in our work, in our daily lives. That's the genesis of 'Ten.8'. It came out of that very small group of people – basically the three of us – pushing it as an issue, trying to get West Midlands Arts to commit towards the idea of a gallery. For some reason we thought that having an identifiable space would enable us to start building a community. In fact Birmingham has never had that. It had it very briefly when I ran the Triangle [arts centre] in the mid-eighties at Aston [university]. But, basically, it has never had that focus. We figured a magazine would be the next best thing, so that's what we did. We thought of it as a vehicle for bringing together a community of people.

So you saw no possibility of a space.

West Midlands Arts talked about it, lots of people went to look at areas that could possibly be potentially turned into galleries – all that kind of bollocks went on; loads of tramping round old buildings. But it was obvious that no one was going to fork out the kind of cash required. Even though, by today's standards, it was a pathetically small amount you were talking about. So we went for the magazine. The first three issues were very much portfolio-based, designed to try and get local talent into there. People like Vanley Burke, local photographers; people who were studying in Birmingham at the time – Paddy Shanahan. Good work. But very portfolio based: very much about, hey: here are the people doing the work, here's the work. Nothing theoretical about it.

How did you contextualise it?

A bit of biographical stuff. It wasn't big stuff at all. We had, in the process of creating the group that West Midlands Arts thought of as fit to run a photography magazine, brought in these other guys, most of who were teaching photography in further and higher education. Of course they were all desperate to get their little pieces published; naively, I didn't realise how important that was for their careers at that point. So there were odd articles like "Atget's Paris" because someone had written a big book. So it was very much of a mishmash – serious in its intent but not deeply focused about what its real objectives were, other than the very broadly expressed one of: hey, it's good to meet.

Where does the name of the title come from?

It came from a sort of drunken session, you know the usual thing where you've got to think of a name. We ended up with two contenders; Viz and Ten.8 because it was the size of a piece of photographic paper. And it just sounded obscure and conceptual enough to be a good title, so it stuck.

It did say "photography".

It did say photography in a rather kind of conventional, technical name. It was used ironically, always. At that stage we had no great ambitions for it. It wasn't as though we were embarking on a project that you felt that it was going to be your life's work. It was one of a number of things we were doing at the time. It was just a fun thing. We met once a week. 'Ten.8' always lived off the back of something else – in most cases the work that Brian and I were doing as designers, then latterly the work we were doing as a publishing house elsewhere. It was a fun thing to do.

Where did you distribute?

It was just distributed locally to start with. It was a 500 print run. Very small scale. But we had ambitions – it always had to be nicely printed, even the first issue the production values were high. We wanted it to be nice.

Did that come from you?

I think that probably came from me. Coming as it were from a "professional" background, you tend to bring production values with you – and particularly photography that I felt had always been badly served in terms of repro. There's no point in saying, we're a photography magazine and then having a dot screen on the pictures so big you might think it was a Lichtenstein print or something. There was always something about production values. The format we ripped off straight from Camerawork. The first three or four issues were produced A3 folding to A4.

In the interim, John, Brian and myself had done our own little photo project. This was called the 'Handsworth self-portraits'. We spent five or six weekends in summer 1979 with a self-portrait booth set up outside our shop; literally on the street. We had a camera and a backdrop against the bay window and the camera on a tripod and had a few signs up in Urdu and Punjabi saying: take your own photographs, free. We got about five or six hundred local people at the weekends taking their own pictures. It turned into a massive project; so interesting. And we had millions and millions of these self-portraits. We decided we would do an issue of 'Ten.8' – and I think this was a turning point (certainly in my conception of what the magazine should be about and could do) from going round and grabbing all the local photographers and whacking their work in the magazine to: here's an issue; what is the issue about self-portraiture? Then the editorial background I came from kicked in and I thought: I'm not just interested in local work – what can we do? Issue number 4 focused on self-portaiture as a genre and was about why people were interested in it; why particularly it was important for issues of stereotyping and the way photographers of one culture might see people of another culture and – inadvertently without being conscious of it – create photographs that match their stereotypical preconceptions. A self-portrait could be designed – theoretically – to undo these preconceptions. And obviously the feminist movement of the late seventies had just discovered self-portraiture as a means of liberating themselves from the male gaze and so on. So we kind of opened the door from being a portfolio magazine, you know: some nice pictures – that one there, than one there ... privileging the photograph, lots of white space, nicely laid out – to a kind of idea that, actually we could use this magazine as a vehicle for investigating lots of interesting ideas. And the first one of which had been kicked up by our own work.

That changed people's perception of the magazine; we distributed it much more widely – because we had international artists involved: i.e. not just people from France or America who happened to be staying in Birmingham, but people who were genuinely living in places like Canada but were doing interesting work that we sought out because it was around a subject area that we were interested in. That changed everybody's idea of the magazine I think. It opened up a different approach. The next issue was A4 book with a spine – which was a format we tried to keep; we didn't always succeed because we couldn't always afford the spine.

What was the frequency?

Roughly quarterly, but… I think the first four issues took about a year and a quarter to produce. We were doing it all in our spare time; Brian and I designed it free, we used all the resources of our studio to create this so it had to be something that was done part-time.

What was the arrangement between the funders and yourselves?

It was a very loose one because they only put up a small amount of money. In those days all funding was done as a guarantee against loss. So if you had a project you went to them and said: this project is going to cost a thousand pounds, we think we can sell 500 copies at 50p each. That will give us £250. Can I have £750 please? And then they paid you bits of money and at the end of the year you had to get your accountant to show your deficit and they paid you the rest. Of course if you had been successful and had sold 1000 copies, and made £500 income they would only have given you £250. So there was no investment in growth, only a disincentive to be successful to avoid your grant going down. That was something that crippled 'Ten.8' at that point. With the demise of 'Camerawork' in London (the perception I had was that it was a real powerhouse of a place that was really churning out, one after the other, very interesting documents about really important issues and then suddenly it stopped). So suddenly we had a sense that maybe we could fill that gap; given that the response to the self-portrait issue had been so enthusiastic, and that we sold in London for the first time and increased our distribution. Suddenly it seemed like the magazine was a massive success and we had a terrific response from people all over the place saying: great to see something happening in Birmingham! It was deeply unfashionable then.

Who was buying it?

No idea. We had no concept of audience. Looking back I think that is one of the big issues about the whole history of than era: not just what we did with 'Ten.8' but all sorts of other people – that we had no concept of audience. The first audience survey we did wasn't until about 1987.

Under duress?

Absolutely under duress! Then we found out that the second favourite hobby of all the readers was gardening. Then the Arts Council was saying to us: if you can do a gardening magazine with photographs you could be very successful. (I wish I had taken their advice.) So, because of the demise of 'Camerawork', which was breaking up, a lot of people turned to 'Ten.8' and we suddenly had this huge influx of people from London. We were going regularly to London because we had to for work reasons. The person who was the catalyst was Ed Barber who had fallen out with Camerawork and saw 'Ten.8' as a new home. He brought loads of ideas and loads of work. He became our London editor for two or three years I suppose, just channelling material up from London and generally breaking up the idea that this was a West Midlands magazine for West Midlands arts photographers and was designed to promote photography in the West Midlands. I lobbied for a gallery – which was one of our initial aims, but all of that went out the window. We thought, we can address the issues: there's a big international audience out there and the sort of issues we're dealing with are really pertinent and nobody else is really dealing with them in quite the way we think we are – or potentially that we would like to deal with them, for we hadn't really done very much. And away we went with the concept that each magazine should be located very much in political issues. The issue after self-portraits was 'restricted practices' which was all about issues facing documentary photographers that were trying to document the truth in a world circumscribed by police activity and lack of access ... We did that with Network agency that had just formed at that point and of course it was full of a lot of people who were already on the fringes of being professional documentary photographers and had moved away from 'Camerawork' because it had become too theoretical. They had created Network and were desperate to promote their kind of vision of "new" British documentary – which wasn't that new but nevertheless was kind of exciting.

You mention the division between thinkers and photographers. Where did you at 'Ten.8' position yourselves in relation to that split?

Personally, I was always fascinated by both. The majority of photographers are fascinating people, although are very limited as thinkers – sometimes very frustrating in that respect; and on the other hand meeting people like John Taylor who were deeply theoretical, and had really no clue about what made an image – their response to an image always seemed to me to be a little bit born of pure art history and they had to apply to it all these things they'd learnt. So I felt that the answer for us was to have a healthy balance between people who were just saying: yeah but this is great photography! And other people who were saying: what's so great about it?

I think having that was one of the strengths of 'Ten.8'.

The editor of 'Creative Camera' throughout most of the seventies and eighties, Peter Turner, believed that he knew instinctively what a good photo was. There must have been an aspect of that attitude at 'Ten.8'.

I think it's fair to say the two examples we had of magazines that we could follow were 'Camerawork' and 'Creative Camera'. 'Creative Camera' we dismissed as being a portfolio-based magazine that didn't attempt to look at any issue beyond: here's a nice set of pictures. I was in touch with it when Colin Osman was in control. He was great because he had the enthusiasm and he had certain things that he was absolutely passionate about. I mean he didn't give a fuck about the audience, because for him it was: this is important and I'm doing it. He did some great issues like the one about 'Drum', amazing stuff. Which was just purely about being an obsessive individual. The magazine was very much run by him then. When Pete was there, there was a small group of people that formed the taste committee, if you like, and you couldn't really get into be a member of that ... Whereas we took a different approach. I think that's always been reflected in Ten.8. We always had very oppositional characters involved in the thing.

There's a lot of denial involved in both the pro-theory and pro-pure photography positions. A lot more common ground exists in fact than people would care to admit.

I agree and that's why I think we took the position to hover between the two, because on one level I was a practitioner; I took photographs, and on another level I was acutely aware what the limitations of these photographs were. So I was quite prepared to entertain all the critiques that were being made. I used to enjoy the chemistry of all that and there were always people taking up these positions. We always had space for anyone to come in and take a very, very radical position and that happened with people like Rhonda Wilson or David A. Bailey who would hijack a whole issue. When you look back at them they kind of zig-zag all over the place, which was chaotic at the time but looking back at it now you think: well all we were doing was being pulled between what were the issues of the day. From an editorial perspective, John Taylor ran it. He had more time and he had more contacts. He was a lecturer ... and there's no question that for a very important period of its development he helped direct the editorial focus and said, look, we should do something about this or do something about that. Even so, on issues that you would say, this is a pure John Taylor issue of 'Ten.8', there was always stuff creeping in that wasn't his. So we were determined not to be a consensual group that said: no, we really know what we think it should be and it should always be this. That always left space for something new to happen without any of it being embarrassing to anyone.

You mentioned proximity to Stourbridge College as important to the magazine. It strikes me that what 'Ten.8' managed to do early on was address the higher education audience. Patrick Shanahan told me that he was inspired by meeting John Taylor at the college and this energy that Patrick saw there must have fed back into the magazine. To what degree was 'Ten.8' regional, national, or academic?

It was always regional – out of the mainstream – and not subject to the same kinds of pressures you get in a place like London. You couldn't afford to have that open forum we had in London because there were too many determined people, too many agendas. We were just a two-hour journey up the M1 that was just far enough for us to see all this stuff [in London] but be able to accommodate it much more easily. It was very important that there was that community in Stourbridge and we were fortunate that it was a golden period for that college at that time. They had some great students and some great lecturers – John obviously and Dick Hebdige was there. He wrote some seminal pieces – the piece about The Face that was in 'Hiding in the Light' appeared in 'Ten.8' first. So there were some really good people around and, in retrospect, they were really, really clever guys. I suppose historically that was just one of those wonderful accidents, and the mere fact of creating a forum like 'Ten.8' enable them all to come together and participate in it in some ways.

What would it have been like if it had been a gallery?

It would have been boring. As it turned out, the magazine was a much more exciting project. We never felt obliged to follow up what we'd done with something exactly the same; so the readers never knew what to expect. It is interesting as well that we did have to work with galleries for some of the more interesting projects. The first really, really giant issue that we did, 'Staying On' (Issue number 16) was the catalogue for an exhibition at the Photographers' Gallery when Alex Noble was curator. That was a huge project on immigrant communities in London that was funded by the Greater London Arts (GLA) and we worked with her and identified writers from each of the communities. CLR James wrote about being an Afro-Caribbean in Britain and there were lots of other good writers and some very interesting photographs. It included Stuart Hall's famous piece about high street photography and the representation of people when they first came over from the Caribbean. We did it for the money, the funding [that was available for a publication to accompany the exhibition]. 'Ten.8' had grown – it sold more, and more went abroad. By then West Midlands Arts was saying, you're not a regional magazine anymore so you have to get your money from the Arts Council. And in those days nobody wanted to put up money for something as difficult to understand as publishing; because you know you have to sort out the money a long time in advance – you're commissioning, you're paying for staff, you've maybe got a lead time of three, four, five months and then you've got three, four, five, six months before people pay up on the sales; so you have sometimes got a cash flow crisis of nearly a year between having a concept for an edition and seeing money returning from your sales. And the Arts Council couldn't deal with that. It wasn't something they could get their heads around.

How did the agenda change after the Arts Council began funding 'Ten.8'?

'Camerawork' had died and they saw us as the natural replacement for the constituency that otherwise would have come and lobbied them. Part of a continuing resentment about 'Ten.8' was that [we were seen as] these geezers from Birmingham [that] have come down and scooped up some cash that should rightfully be for London-based projects. There was always that.

Resentment from whom?

Anybody who was asking for any money.

Around 1980, after 'Creative Camera' was rescued by the Arts Council, photography magazines were expected to get revenue from the growing academic sector.

We had in fact, inadvertently, segued into that whole market. As you identified, the growth of those photography courses, the need for some kind of theory to be taught, and some issues about representation, and we were suddenly in the midst of that because that was exactly what we were doing – without identifying it as what we should be doing.

At what point did you realise that 'Ten.8' was locked into higher education?

I suppose not until we got computerised, about 1986. Then we created a database of all our subscribers and you could kind of interrogate it and sort it by kind and all that sort of stuff. Then you realised if you didn't have institutional sales you wouldn't exist. Of course by then – like 'Creative Camera' – we were being bought by virtually every reputable photography course everywhere.

Despite its stress on issues and so on, 'Ten.8' was always very sensitive about how the pictures were presented too. Was there an internal discussion about design and presentation?

There were discussions about that but there was a kind of polarity around that issue … I just didn't see what the contradiction was between saying, here is something on this page that will give you enormous pleasure – just looking at it – and at the same time can raise lots of troubling questions in your mind, and on this page here we'll talk about these troubling questions. That doesn't mean to say that we can't enjoy the troubling questions in a purely kind of visual sense. When we did the 'Digital Dialogues' and 'Critical Decade' issues in the nineties that was absolutely what I was trying to do. I think that bit of 'Ten.8' definitely comes from me: that we mustn't disregard the picture but we mustn't privilege the picture above the words…

Affiliations with other magazines besides 'Camerawork'?

We used to get everything. 'Photofile', but it came later. And there was 'Afterimage' or 'Third Text' that were just deeply theoretical that we were always intrigued with. But there is at the heart of this what you could say was a purely journalistic project where you take something that is actually quite complex and try and make it – not simplified – but comprehensive; give people routes into it. So if you're routed that you are a visual person then the magazine has to be visual. And if your route in is words and you are an ideas person then we will want to give you substantial text. But we don't want you to feel that it's one thing or the other.

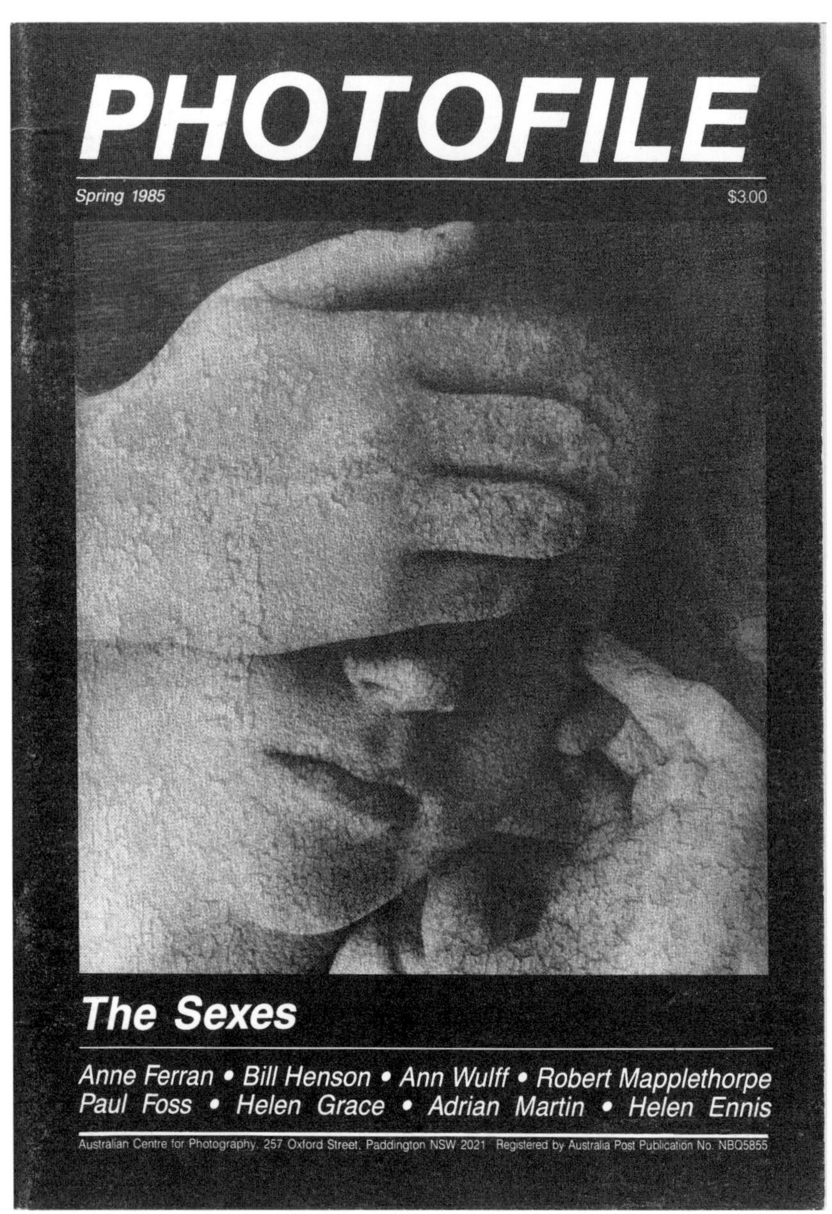
PHOTOFILE
Spring 1985
$3.00
The Sexes
Anne Ferran • Bill Henson • Ann Wulff • Robert Mapplethorpe
Paul Foss • Helen Grace • Adrian Martin • Helen Ennis
Australian Centre for Photography, 257 Oxford Street, Paddington NSW 2021 Registered by Australia Post Publication No. NBQ5855

Geoffrey Batchen: *Photofile*

'Photofile' was founded in 1983 as the newsletter for the activities of the Australian Centre for Photography in Sydney, Australia. Soon afterwards it became a semi-autonomous critical journal and is still publishing today, internationally. Geoffrey Batchen was editor for seven issues between 1985 and 1986.

David Brittain: What was the cultural magazine sector like in Australia before you began editing 'Photofile'?

Geoffrey Batchen: When I started as an undergraduate student, 'Art and Australia' was the only magazine there was; it had some reviews, but in general it was a glossy promotional magazine; it published a lot of expository essays on individual artists and it covered some historical exhibitions. It had a lot of colour. It was a very attractive, handsome sort of magazine, but it had no critical capacity whatsoever.

Were you involved with that prior to 'Photofile'?

I was involved with another magazine, called 'Art Network', from the second issue on, even though I was only an undergraduate at the time. 'Art Network' was started by a bunch of artists as a counter to 'Art and Australia', and it emphasized grass-roots arts activism such as artist-run spaces and galleries and non-commercial art practices of various kinds. The title, 'Art Network', tells you a lot about it. Its rival was 'Art & Text' ('Art Network' was published in Sydney and 'Art & Text' was published in Melbourne). Both of them started out of nothing and then attracted government funding. One represented this kind of leftist network-public art/bill board kind of aesthetic and 'Art & Text' represented the hottest post-modern theory and all that. One issue of 'Art Network' was devoted to photography. I became involved in 'Photofile' when I came to work for the Australian Centre for Photography (ACP) in Sydney in 1984. I took over as editor after the journal had already been around for two years. The issues from these first two years of 'Photofile' were based on the style of 'Afterimage'; they had that same newspaper fold-out format. 'Photofile', 'Art Network' and 'Art & Text' each represented quite a distinct voice in critical approach. These magazines were fellow travellers at the time; we were all friends and a number of people wrote for all three of them. It was a bit of a mutual admiration society. It was also a time when a lot of magazines were being published (the Australia Council, the Federal Arts Funding Body, decided that there should be an art magazine published in each state) and criticism was perhaps the most important aspect of the art world.

Did you have an editorial or management committee at 'Photofile'?

When I took over 'Photofile', along with this newspaper format, one of the things I inherited was a committee. It was basically an editorial committee that was formed out of members of the ACP but I inherited a different one from the earlier one. Mine happened to consist of really all the best young art photographers in Sydney at the time – people like Anne Ferran, Marian Marrison, Helen Grace, Jacky Redgate. They were the hottest photo artists of the eighties. I was very fortunate to have such good people because they supported me in general as I made changes to the magazine (although it wasn't like they gave me a rubber stamp). The way it would work was I put together an issue's worth of copy – but always had enough copy for one and a half issues. So they would read all the copy; they'd come to my house and there was a rule that they would have to have frozen chocolate biscuits waiting for them. This was the deal, like a group joke. Then we would basically discuss all the copy that had come in for that issue. I would have written up a potential contents page basically prioritizing what I would have liked included, but inevitably, they changed it. There would have to be a consensus decision in other words. Often they decided they preferred this piece or they wanted it even if it was badly written. Then I would just need to re-edit it into some sort of shape. So they were very much active in the whole process – which was great for me because at the time I knew nothing about photography. When I applied for the job as editor of Photofile, I remember the director coming back from the meeting after the interview and saying, "Well, I'm giving you the job but you better not let me down." That made me a little nervous. What had I just got myself into?

What was your speciality?

I had a three-year degree in architecture – it was a six-year degree but I had the first half; after three years they gave you a Bachelor of Science. I had to repeat one subject and so I also started an arts degree at Sydney University, so for one year I was juggling two degrees. The arts degree in Australia is the umbrella under which you then major in art history. So I got a four-year honours degree in art history. I also had this architecture background. I had a graduate scholarship to do a PhD – that's what funded my involvement with Photofile basically. I was living on the scholarship but I never wrote a word of my PhD during the two years that I edited 'Photofile'. But I could live on that; 'Photofile' paid almost nothing, maybe it was like $500 an issue. Which was about $2000 a year sometimes. So I had this fellowship plus this small income from 'Photofile'. I did seven issues over two years. Always with this same editorial group and with the same designer, a guy called Allan Martin. He was also editing Tribune, the communist party newspaper, so it was an interesting experience. I knew Allan through a mutual friend and took him on as a designer. I would put all the copy together – in those pre-computer days it had to go to the typesetters, get carefully copy edited then get taken back to the typesetters; magazine editing was really laborious in those days. I'm sure you would remember these long strips of text that he would patch onto a waxed page. It was done at the communist party headquarters, so like nine or 10 on a Sunday night I would get a call: "OK you can come down and look at it." So I would drive down and park somewhere – totally in the middle of the city – and then bang the secret knock on the bottom of the door of communist party headquarters. That was 1985-86.

How much knowledge about photography, generally, was there at the time?

I had almost none. But I had just done the Whitney programme in 1983 and 84 so I'd met and knew Barbara Kruger and Craig Owens and Benjamin Buchloh and all those kinds of people. And at that time in New York, at the high point of the post-modern debates, photography was at the forefront of it as a mode of reproduction whose originality was contested and so on. All the best criticism in New York was about photography of one kind or another or it was about paintings, like those by David Salle, that were informed by photographic imagery. So I came back to Sydney full of all this stuff but knowing nothing about the history of photography. Indeed the Australian Centre for Photography took a huge risk by giving someone, who knew so little, this job. Like most of these situations, you learn a lot on the job. By the time I'd done my second or third issue I knew at least something about it. 'Photofile' was the only national photography magazine so instantly I was thrust into the centre of this community.

What I came to see was that the "photography community" was a very fragmented one because you have a bunch of people whose every question is about lenses and f-stops, a bunch of people who are basically conceptual artists with cameras in their hands, then you have a variety of people in between. The magazine, in its earlier manifestation, had been more like a newsletter; it had been edited by photographers and I was, of course, not a photographer. Their magazine had long interviews with photographers and curators; it was very chatty and anecdotal and what I wanted to do was a magazine of criticism. So the committee and I and the designer decided to completely change the format. We had to have the capacity to compete with these other magazines – like 'Art & Text' and 'Art Network'. The newspaper format was not going to allow that. So the first thing we did was to change it to this A4-sized format. Allan Martin redesigned it and the cover was black and it had a much more aggressive sans serif face on it and it actually sold itself on the basis of who was writing within it. The names of its writers were becoming famous. And the kind of photography that we chose to foreground was totally different from the early magazine, which had been much more documentary-oriented; now we were into this post-modern, feminist conceptual stuff.

Another decision we made early on was that it was to be a magazine of criticism not a magazine of photography. One of the magazines that had preceded 'Photofile' was an older one called 'Light Vision', published in Melbourne. It was a folio magazine and was therefore somewhat despised by people like us because it emphasised the pictures over the text. Basically it was a promotional glossy and beautiful magazine and we didn't want that. Some famous Australian photographers, like Max Dupain, ended up writing in to complain about the poor reproduction quality in 'Photofile' and that the text was allowed to dominate the pictures. That was deliberate policy on our part for the magazine was supposed to be about criticism, it wasn't about the beautiful photograph, per se. Of course what we had was the best reproduction quality we could afford anyway; it wasn't as if we had much choice in the matter. We felt that it was still better than the newspaper format had allowed in 'Photofile's' previous manifestation. The magazine prospered greatly under this change. We printed a lot more text than before. Its coverage of Australian photography became more and more comprehensive. The design became tighter and tighter as Allan and I had a better sense of what we were about. It brought people in who hadn't written about Australian photography before. One of the things I said in my retrospective writings about the magazine (see, for example, "After Postmodernism," in 'What is this thing called Photography?: Australian Photography 1975-1985') was that it shifted photography from its own ghetto into the broader cultural and artistic debates in Australia at the time. That was one of my functions in my two years as editor of 'Photofile'.

Yes, editors soon find that the photography community is fragmented. Very often these different constituencies will begin to identify with different magazines.

The ACP as an institution (comprising studios, a gallery and a magazine) constantly struggled with this problem. The studios were fine, you could do classes there and a lot of well known photographers taught night classes there – but they were basically teaching kids and members of the community who wanted to learn about technique. The magazine, on the other hand, was this hot-shot post-modern photo criticism magazine and I would be surprised if a single student from the workshops ever read it. Or was interested in it. They were out photographing their nude girlfriends or landscapes and here we were talking about theories of sexuality and the body or something like that. And the gallery – which of course was the public face of this institution – had this constant struggle too because of these multiple constituencies; if they showed post-modern photography then all the documentary people who set the gallery up in the first place felt that they were being left out. If they showed documentary then all of the young hotshots thought, it's too fuddy-duddy an organisation for them and they'd go elsewhere. It has never managed to resolve that, it still pleases nobody. But I think the courage of the editorial committee and myself was we said, "Well this magazine will just be what we want it to be. It won't be all things to all people, and therefore satisfying none."

The magazine was way more advanced or avant-garde, if you like, than the gallery ever was. But the gallery had to catch up because the magazine was creating a national profile for the institution that the institution didn't otherwise fulfil. So the gallery had to exhibit these artists (that we published) and do different kinds of exhibitions than it had previously, and pay more attention to a critical profile within its exhibition programme.

Did any go abroad?

Yeah. San Francisco Camerawork had the magazine for sale. But we never got any money out of it – we wrote these off. So there was the odd distribution overseas but it was small.

In Britain the early eighties was the beginning of the expansion of photography within the higher education system. It was hoped that this sector would become a serious market for "serious" photography magazines. Was there a parallel in Australia?

Like I said, 'Photofile' to some degree developed its own market, so it may be by the time you're into the third or fourth and fifth year of the magazine there was a growing constituency of students. When I went through the Whitney programme, in 1983, there was virtually no post-modern art theory in Australia. There was no French criticism; I'd never heard of the names Jacques Derrida or Roland Barthes. When I came back it was everywhere. 'Art & Text' was publishing all this stuff; the month I came back Baudrillard was in town to give a lecture. And theory was suddenly hot! One of the effects of that was that every art department – probably in the country – developed new classes that were called "critical theory", whatever that was. And this theory became the staple diet of every undergraduate student. Before then it didn't exist. There might have been the odd seminar about criticism, but it was probably not what we now think of as criticism.

In a sense 'Photofile' was part of, and also contributed to, this growing profile for this new type of teaching that came under the rubric of critical theory. So it may be that three or four years into the magazine there was a new constituency thinking in these same terms that would have been looking for a magazine that spoke that language. At that time the market for us was the young generation of art photographers, recent graduates. So I would say that was the readership I had in mind; they were often the writers too. As an editor you're often blundering in the dark in that respect; you don't quite know who your readers are.

The other constituency that 'Photofile' had to constantly keep in mind was the national one. ACP was the Australian Centre for Photography and 'Photofile' explicitly had to cater for a national audience. At the start of the magazine we had a section devoted to the regions – which meant anything outside of Melbourne or Sydney. So part of my mission as editor was to make the magazine more national, building a constituency outside of Sydney, finding writers outside of Sydney – so in terms of this imagined audience, that search for national content drove a lot of the biggest efforts of the magazine. Finding one person who could write in Adelaide, for example, was a huge thing. The quality of the writing was not the first priority, it was representative coverage we were looking for.

Was that a condition of grant aid?

It became one more and more. Yet how could the ACP be a national organisation and have a gallery in Sydney? How could they pretend to be doing anything for people in Perth? The magazine was seen by the institution as one way for the organisation to fulfil its national obligations. By being cheap and mobile it could actually represent Australian photography in a way that the gallery never really did.

We have talked about the fragmentation of the magazine's constituency over different aesthetics or politics; but there's a regional aspect to this issue that was harder to overcome. Good documentary photographers can still appreciate avant-garde art photography to some degree and vice versa – but Melbourneites find it harder to appreciate a magazine that comes from Sydney. On a personal level it was a huge struggle because you would be dealing with Melbourne writers who were always suspicious of you. We decided, as a Sydney-based editorial committee, that we would just have features and a review section and there would no longer be a special section devoted to what's happening in Melbourne or Adelaide. At that point the Melbourne section was written by a guy called Bernie O'Regan, who was incredibly important to the magazine's profile in Melbourne. He would write a little news column, very chatty, anecdotal. He was a photographer. So he was a bit of a leftover from the first manifestation of the magazine and, although he was a very nice guy, his voice just didn't fit the new Photofile regime. So eventually he got pissed off and dropped out and became important in the formation of the [Melbourne-based] Victoria Centre for Photography.

That's the sad thing – all these magazines begin in a bubble of collective energy and then they end up becoming more and more similar because the state puts more and more restrictions on them. You have to do so many things to make you nationally representative and that actually dilutes the original mission of each magazine. So we all felt the pressure – you had to be representative, you had to be national, you had to do this and do that in order to secure the funding and that meant that every magazine felt the pressure to become more like each other

.

Did the photography people who didn't read 'Photofile' have any other platform?

Not really. But, despite what I've been saying I should emphasise that this was a deliberately pluralist magazine. I remember adding up the stats and I think 40 per cent of our writers were photographers, for example. You're desperate for good content, and if I got good stuff that was documentary then I didn't care as long as it was good stuff. But the writing we were looking for was not about appreciation, it was about criticism and that was the difference.

The other thing I still feel is that the magazine at that period educated its market; these younger voices shifted the orientation of photography – for better or worse. It changed the way photography was regarded within the art world.

Some of the best artists in Australia then were photographers. In fact they wanted to be called artists and some of them refused to exhibit in the Australian Centre for Photography because they didn't want to be thought of as purely photographers. So 'Photofile' followed that trend but also reinforced it with its own orientation. When it started I never wanted the magazine to be an art magazine (I wanted it to be more like Ten.8) – but I could never find writers who were willing to write about non-art topics. With my own work now I still struggle with this. I'm trying – at my own pathetic little level – to shift that orientation again. It was better writing that found its way into 'Photofile' – but it was still all about art.

Was there a model in mind when you began editing?

A good question. Because I knew nothing about photography, it wasn't as if I was particularly familiar with other photography magazines or anything like that. Interestingly – this will show how limited I was in my thinking – the page design of the magazine was actually based on the 'Manchester Guardian Weekly'. I used to read it every week fanatically and I remember ripping out a page and taking it to Allan the designer while we were redesigning 'Photofile'. If you actually look at the design of an issue from this period you can see much of it was taken straight from the Guardian. I was almost blissfully ignorant of any photo magazine anywhere else in the world. So 'Art & Text' and 'Art Network' were the two Australian magazines that were the biggest influence on me personally, because I knew them already.

There were other Australian precedents for 'Photofile' – such as 'Working Papers on Photography'. They published Sekula's first essay on documentary photography. There was 'Halide', which was put out by students at Sydney College of the Arts. There were only a few issues of that. Frankly, I didn't know any of these older magazines really because I wasn't part of the photography scene. That enabled me, as an editor, to break with tradition in the way that someone who was on the photo scene might not have been able to do. I just trampled over that tradition because I didn't know it. That's just the way it worked out.

'Photofile' was done very cheaply. We're talking really cheap. Once upon a time I had all the budgets and if you looked at what we spent it was a laughable amount of money. Policy-wise – as a requirement of state funding, but also a 'Photofile' policy – it was a requirement that we paid our writers, but we also paid our photographers. So anyone who got reproduced in the magazine was paid a reproduction fee – which no other magazine was doing at the time. It was a piddley amount, $50 or something, but it was a good policy, I think. If we reproduced an image in the magazine we regarded it as editorial content – just like text. These were also the days when you went to a lot of trouble to ensure that 40-50 per cent of contributors were women. I don't think now you really have to do that because they just are. I told you I used to give the editorial committee a contents page of each issue, but I also had a breakdown of gender, region, the ratio of photographers and non-photographers who were contributing. So we deliberately had an affirmative action policy to make sure we had women contributing and also photographers. As an editor it was a huge amount of work because photographers are sometimes not very literate, so most of my labour went into rewriting text into legible English. I don't regret it; I think it was an important policy and in terms of the issue of constituency, you wanted to be able to say to people who complained: "Look, half of our contributors are photographers! You're reading your peers, not your critics." That was another continuing concern. The women thing worked itself out because the best art photographers at the time were women and a lot of the writers were women. So region, gender and practice were the three categories that were constantly being talked about by the editorial committee.

What foreign titles could you buy?

Most of the British magazines were in the ACP library, I think there was 'Creative Camera' and 'Camerawork'. Because of the close relationship between Australia and Britain (in contrast to the US) we knew what was going on there. Helen Grace, one of my committee members, was one of the Hackney Flashers. So she knew Jo Spence and that whole scene and she brought that back to us. So members of the editorial committee were better educated than me; they were photographers after all. I knew nothing about the history of photography, about the Bauhaus or the 'Film und Foto' exhibition or anything. And maybe that's better. For, in Australia – because it's a provincial culture – there's a tendency to want to imitate your betters. Fortunately, I just didn't know my betters.

To what degree was 'Photofile' independent of the ACP gallery?

The short answer is the magazine more or less ignored the gallery. It bore no relationship to the exhibition programme. Apart from the input of the editorial committee, it was pretty much a one-man band. I spent 24 hours a day, seven days a week doing this magazine. I literally hand-delivered copies to each bookstore in Sydney. I picked them up again at the end of the month. I picked up the money, I did all the accounting, I solicited all the advertising. It was just me working on the content, and then I would hand it to the designer. The editor did everything. I often designed the ads, wrote the copy for the ads. I went from bookshop to bookshop, literally begging them to take the magazine. So running Photofile was definitely a labour of love. We felt that there was a political mission to the whole project. About which now, all these years later, I have more doubts about than I did then. At the time it seemed that everything we did mattered – and it did matter then. In the sense that there were these different constituencies within the photography community and it was almost as if you were landing a blow, each time you put out an issue, to this old notion of the photograph as a transparent window onto something.

So you felt you were the shock troops against Modernism?

Exactly. And Modernism wasn't just art. Modernism was Reagan and Thatcher and their equivalents in Australia. If you could shock the art community out of its complacency you felt like you were doing good work. It was interesting to live through the nineties when Clinton was in power in the US. Your guy is in power yet nothing has changed! It was the same in Australia, the Labour party was in power for a long time and in fact nothing significantly changed. So you begin to develop doubts about the mission you had in the early eighties. But at the time those of us involved in the magazine scene felt like we were fellow soldiers; there was a real sense of camaraderie and that we were doing something important. And we were. We did have an impact. We changed things, even if only a little bit.

Who were your peers then?

I had come back to Australia inspired by Craig Owens particularly and by Barbara Kruger and Martha Rosler and Mary Kelly, who were all writing as well as making things (the 'October' crowd at the time were our models). Now, of course they're the opposition. They are now the establishment. But at the time 'October' was having this huge impact – you ran down the street to read the latest Craig Owens essay, it was like your brains were exploding out of your head to read it! Now that I'm an old guy and I go to conferences here and there, I have students sort of saying the same thing about books they're reading and it reminds me of what it is to be a student. It's a great time in your life when you can read things and feel literally that your life has changed overnight as a result of reading this essay. When I was a student it was a period when Australian education was free. I remember attending a class on Lacan. It went for three hours from six till nine one night a week. And there were students from three other universities who drove across Sydney to be at this class and yet there were only two people actually enrolled and that would be in a class of 20 or 30 people who regularly turned up. When education was free, you could afford to learn for its own sake.

That's what informed all of this – this constituency of theory heads. At the time, Australian intellectuals were constrained by this union working-class leftist, Marxist tradition we inherited from Britain but we soon began to question that. Marxists seemed conservative and out of step with the times. French theory, as it was called, was not just king; it was god. There was no point having a conversation with people who hadn't read Barthes, or hadn't read Foucault and hadn't read Derrida. Your whole world view shifted as a result of reading that stuff. And 'Photofile' was about embodying that shift. And proselytising it to the rest of the community. It was an almost theological passion we had for it.

And the magazine was full of that language and that was why it ostracised a certain element of one's constituency. We saw ourselves as far in advance of what Brits were doing at the time at the level of art practice and at the level of criticism. Whereas I'd been brought up on Burgin and Tagg and that kind of tentative step into Foucault from Marx, we now looked to Americans like Craig Owens. They were talking the talk, or so it seemed. In Australia, postmodern theory actually first came to us through gay liberation magazines, that were the first to publish essays informed by Foucault and similar theorists. So, for Australian scholars, French theory was always politicised, it was always part of the gay liberation movement. For Marxists there was a debate about whether this stuff was apolitical, or simply rhetorical. For a younger generation, though, it was always grounded in sexual politics. We just assumed from the outset that all these people – Foucault, Derrida, and so on – were political animals. When I came to the US, I was quite surprised how conservatively it was framed there – as opposed to how politically active it was in Australia. So again, editing a magazine like 'Photofile', even though it was about art photography – in our heads it was also a form of activist politics.

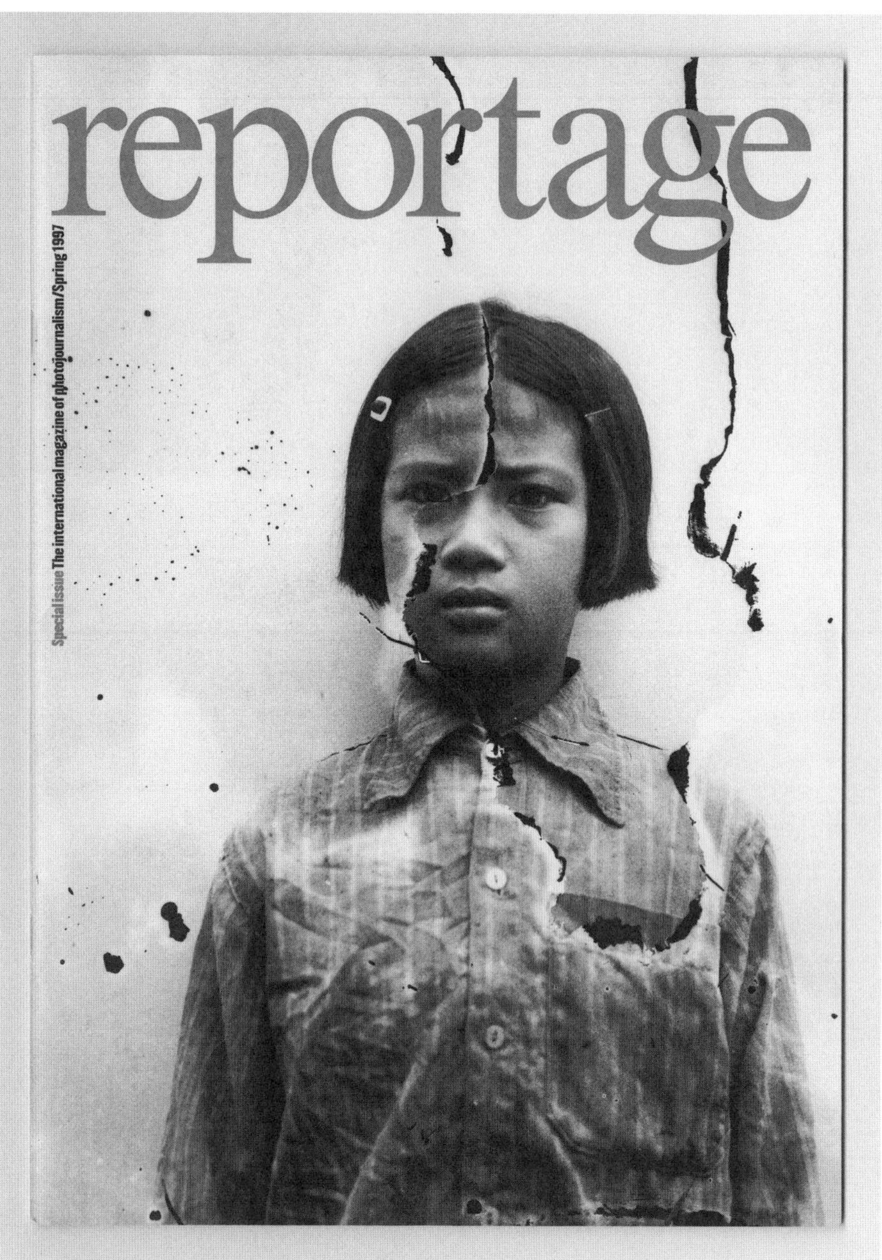
reportage
Special Issue The international magazine of photojournalism/Spring 1997

Colin Jacobson: *Reportage*

The privately-financed 'Reportage' appeared in 1995 as a showcase for the art of the journalistic picture essay. Though the title was forced to close in 2000, it maintains a web presence. Colin Jacobson, the founder-editor, has a background as a magazine picture editor.

David Brittain: Summarise your career previous to 'Reportage'.

Colin Jacobson: I entered journalism when I was in my late twenties, thirty, after working on research projects. I worked on a couple of very large social surveys, LSE [London School of Economics] and University of Essex-type surveys and I was really just a minion doing questionnaires, processing and things like that. I was quite bored with that. Then, quite by chance, I heard of and got a short-term contract to be a researcher on a project for the 'Sunday Times' magazine called 'The Facts of Life' – it was a part-work about science and medicine. It was one of those totally random things; I fell into this position by chance because somebody else had fallen out of it. I found that part of the job was picture research and I really got into that very quickly. And I just loved it. I had grown up with visual things around me because my dad worked for 'Picture Post' as a writer and before that was associate editor on 'Lilliput'. So there was a magazine tradition but it never really clicked that that was work somehow. I went through the academic treadmill and graduated with a degree in politics, philosophy and economics. And it was as if there were some residual visual memories in me of 'Picture Post' coming through the door and 'Lilliput' and so on. But I took to it like a duck to water. So, by a series of lucky accidents my contract was extended over four years at the 'Sunday Times Magazine' where I basically learnt the whole magazine business. They only had one picture researcher on the magazine and I became that person, and I was working with very talented people like Michael Rand and Bruce Bernard who was picture editor. Just by osmosis, I learnt a huge amount about what picture journalism was all about. That was about 1972-1976. Then I got the job at 'The Economist' as picture editor. It sounds like an oxymoron, being picture editor at that magazine, but it was the time when they had the idea that they wanted to make it more visual.

If you were doing picture research during Bruce Bernard's era was it mostly historical material you were after?

A lot of historical stuff. I remember we did a special issue on the queen Mum's something or other birthday and it drove me mad. But the best thing about 'Sunday Times Magazine' culture at that time was that they would give you freedom. For instance, I was researching a story about gypsies ... but I discovered just by chance (this was pre-internet) that there was an archive at the University of Liverpool about travellers, so I got the OK to go to Liverpool for two or three days and look at the archive; and I came back with some great pictures, and they used one on a double-page spread. And that was considered to be value for money; if you could send a researcher away to come back with a picture that made a double-page spread – it was cheaper than commissioning a photographer to do a contemporary story! It could be contemporary stories or historical stories. If you analyse any colour supplement from the sixties onwards you will probably find that a proportion of the content was historical or researched, not commissioned. Particularly now. So anyway I got head-hunted onto this weird magazine called Now!. Again that was an unlikely place to find yourself – very, very right wing... On the picture front, they left us alone basically – providing that the subject matter wasn't UK politics. You could do hardcore stories about earthquakes in Algeria and Lech Walesa in the shipyards in Poland. It was the first time I got seriously into working with photographers. There was a big enough budget to buy stories and to commission stories. That lasted two years and we did some good stories, you know. It was in the middle of the magazine surrounded by all this crap about politics. The picture sections were basically apolitical. That was a fast learning curve about news photography.

That is when you first started commissioning.

Around that time, 1979. I hadn't really had much experience working with photographers until that time. After 'Now!' folded dramatically one day, after two years, I did six years on 'The Observer Magazine'. I was called picture features editor and was basically in charge of the whole picture side of the magazine. That was when I really got into the commissioning side... Then I got head-hunted by the 'Independent Magazine'. I got rung up by Alexander Chancellor who was going to be the editor and it was between me and another couple of people and I was lucky enough to get it. And I worked there for six years. The first three were really the most productive part of my magazine experience.

What made that experience so different?

Partly because there was a sort of respect. There was a kind of unequivocal respect. Alexander was one of these editors who, if he'd appointed you, would let you get on with it if you could justify what you were doing. Sometime after he left the magazine, he told a colleague that he felt he had given the picture desk far too much freedom. But we had a certain kind of freedom and the main picture story was right in the middle of the magazine, uninterrupted by ads which was pretty unprecedented.

Was that in contrast to usual magazine practice?

If you go back to the sixties and analyse magazines there are always problems with ads interrupting the flow of stories. We didn't have that problem, we had six to eight spreads regularly without an ad. Alexander had got this agreement that you could have ads at the front and ads at the back but not in the middle. So it was a very eclectic picture section. I looked at a lot of people's personal projects; someone might have been working away on a story about a village in Mexico or whatever for five years and thought they didn't have a hope in hell of having it published in a magazine. But we did it. Things like that. We did a fantastic story about executions in China. When the Russians went into Afghanistan on New Year's Eve I was dispatched to Paris to grab the pictures from a French agency. It was a very unusual experience – but unfortunately it didn't last because Alexander got recruited to the 'New Yorker'. In their wisdom the "troika" (Andreas Whittam Smith, Stephen Glover and Matthews Symonds) running 'The Independent' decided to bring in this guy John Walsh as editor. His remit was obviously to turn it more into a conventional colour magazine; he wanted models on the front. He was obsessed with Elle Macpherson. He was always saying: Can we have a picture of Elle Macpherson? I always kind of resisted it by not doing it and he didn't pick up the gauntlet. So I had another unhappy couple of years that were counter-productive, because if you don't get on with your editor then it's always going to end in tears. And I think it fell away that magazine, journalistically. It just didn't have the confidence.

As I recall the 'Independent Magazine' had the reputation for being the place of choice for young photographers with personal projects.

It was for a while.

I would refer young photographers to you at the 'Independent Magazine'. Were you aware of your reputation as a supporter of new photography?

It was a nice position to be in because nobody else was doing a lot of these stories. And we usually treated photographers with respect. They usually had at least six pages, sometimes more.

Was this the first time you'd seen this side of photography – the unseen, unedited project?

Maybe on 'The Observer Magazine' a bit. It was probably the first time things came out the woodwork at you and you realised there was a whole world out there of photographers doing interesting things ...

Were you aware of participating in a wider world of photography, outside magazine publishing?

The 'Independent Magazine' stage was a time when I started thinking that there was that world out there that I hadn't been too involved with, of Arles and Perpignan photography festivals. And I definitely made an attempt to get into that world of going to Arles. In Arles 91 I made a 17-minute audio visual about the fall of Thatcher, with music and so on; so I kind of became on the international scene after that, then I started getting on the World Press [Photo] jury as well...

Looking at portfolios?

At the 'Independent Magazine' there was less time to see new portfolios. Like all magazines you tend to start working with a stable of photographers that you trust. A lot of commissioning I did was with the Network photographers agency who seemed to have that slightly left-of-centre, humanist outlook on the world. I wanted to work with the younger photographers, not the well-established Magnum photographers.

That's the background. What motivated you to want to set up 'Reportage'?

Well, if I am brutally frank, it was a knee-jerk reaction to what was happening at the 'Independent Magazine'. I was probably not the only person to feel this, but I felt betrayed by the way that the magazine was being undermined. OK, all magazines need to change and grow and move in different directions, but to appoint somebody so diametrically different to Alexander Chancellor was a conscious policy on the part of "the troika" and it just seemed quite insulting to the team; and I wasn't the only one to feel conned. There weren't many other people doing the thing we were doing – that thing we talked about, finding this slightly hidden work. And I wanted to find a way of continuing to show the work that was out there still. It also coincided with the fact that – for reasons I'd completely forgotten – I got this massive tax rebate from my extremely able accountant and it was about twenty grand. I don't want to sound noble but I thought: I better put my money where my mouth is (I'd been sounding off about things) so I decided to put that money into 'Reportage'. Having decided that, it was all far too quick a process. I talked to Simon Estherson the design consultant and he put me in touch with Nick Barlow who was on the managing and production side of 'Tate' magazine. But I was incredibly naïve. I just talked to Nick and put a few figures on that back of an envelope and thought it was going to be alright. We never had a proper business plan – if we'd had a proper business plan we'd have never done it. Everybody would have told you it was completely mad. I remember Chancellor telling me "You're mad to put your own money in it". I thought, well, who else will? I did try and approach a few people... But nobody was interested. Basically it was all happening in a bit of a rush. I got a quote from a far-too-expensive printer called Balding and Mansell who were the crème de la crème. In retrospect these were crazy decisions but the momentum was going by that time and Simon Estherson had a good relationship with Balding and Mansell, which meant it was going to be quality. We wanted good quality. Somehow I convinced myself – or had been convinced – that if we could maintain a subscription base of 3000 it would work – it wouldn't make any money but it would pay for itself. And I thought: well, this whole world of photography I am involved with now, you go to Paris and you meet photographers from America who think 'The Independent' is great – and you think: 2000 subscribers: it's going to be so easy. But how wrong I was! Of course the problem is – and this is pre-email – in your first year you might get quite a high proportion of people re-subscribing, then the second year it all falls away. Every time I sent a reminder letter it cost about a thousand quid in postage. It was totally uneconomical. It started off with just over 3000 subscriptions but by the end of year two it was down 2000.

Well, 2000 wasn't so bad.

It wasn't bad. But the production costs were far too high. We stuck with Balding and Mansell for the first period of the magazine. We had two lives, there were about 14 issues in total. The first one was June 95. That was two years, then there was a hiatus and the last one came out about 2000. The first incarnation stopped when we ran out of money, the second time we started I started working with a publisher I knew in Holland and we did manage to keep it going for another two years. Then we ran out of money. Just to say frankly, it was a bit of vanity publishing; but it was as much an emotional as a rational decision. Something like this needed to be done.

Could it be described as altruism on your part?

That's a bit heavy ... I was beginning to get a reputation as a good picture editor and I wanted to find a way to continue that because I could see the writing on the wall at 'The Independent'. This was the time when lifestyle journalism and celebrity journalism were dominating magazines more and more and I had a strong instinct that there was never going to be mainstream magazines available to work for like the old 'Sunday Times', like the 'Independent Magazine' from that particular publishing era. So it was a mixture of things ... A lot of photographers I knew who were at that time getting to their mid-career stage. They were of a generation who had started with high hopes about the role of photojournalism at the beginning of the Thatcher era and by the end of the nineties after Thatcher was gone, the kind of left-of-centre impetus was falling away; they were getting older and had mortgages and suddenly one of their main points of contact was disappearing.

People such as?

People like Barry Lewis, Mike Abrahams, Mike Goldwater, people like that who are really good photographers who never quite had the celebrity status of some photographers who were around.

What was 'Reportage's' mission?

Partly a platform for myself, partly a platform for photographers I respected, partly a platform for that sort of hidden world of people who had work and didn't know where to take it. Partly there was an element of "the struggle". Within British magazines the written word is dominant. There were always double standards within the budgets about who got the biggest slice of the cake in magazines. I always felt that we weren't able to compete on a level playing field in terms of the amount of commissioning we could do. Even the 'Independent Magazine' were happy to pay someone like Gore Vidal huge amounts of money to write a piece, but if you wanted to send a photographer off for one tenth of that it was a struggle. One of the more – in retrospect stupid and naive – bases for 'Reportage' was that it would be dominated by visual journalism, and that there would be very little text. That was part of my knee-jerk reaction to what was going on, which I now feel was a big error because one of the problems was that the magazine didn't have enough text at times. We slowly did get into commissioning writers. But at the time it was: got to find a platform for these picture stories come what may and if it's only 250 words or 500 words then that's enough.

So the mission was to try to continue that tradition – that classical tradition that I am still not ashamed of – of promoting self-contained picture stories that stand on their own even though they require text to provide context, but they have an essence of their own and can be understood at a visual level with the help of context. The magazines were giving up on it. In the last decade, formerly highly respected magazines, like the 'Sunday Times', through a slow process of erosion, have virtually given up on picture story-telling.

I remember being very struck by the fact that the pictures were all black and white. Why did story-telling have to be black and white?

At the time I definitely felt that it had to be black and white, but I have moved on quite a lot.

You were using colour when you were at the 'Independent Magazine'.

Not much. In fact I remember when I was interviewed by Alexander Chancellor for the job he said to me, confidentially: How would you feel about a magazine that was only black and white? I went: fantastic!

Why were you so keen on black and white?

I think it was the 'Picture Post' tradition I grew up with, nostalgia, but also I associated the erosion of good picture journalism with the colour magazine mentality, that somehow colour stories never hit the mark in the way black-and-white ones did.

So another part of the mission was to cultivate a black and white practice?

Partly. A lot of the people whose work I had been feeding off, if you like, were also working in black and white and there was something purist about it.

Interesting in the mid-nineties that there was still this defence of black and white.

I don't think it's changed hugely. If you ask a lot of photojournalists what their medium of choice would be I think a lot of them will still say black and white. Now of course, it doesn't mean the same – you don't have to consciously put black and white film in your camera, you can shoot digitally and change it. Whether it is just creative fantasy or arrogance, I somehow think that black and white is real and colour is flim-flam. But looking back, it was for economic reasons that the magazine was doomed to failure – not whether it was in black and white or colour. And I have to say this for the record: that I do feel slightly ashamed or embarrassed that I was asking subscribers to commit themselves to a magazine which any businessman would have predicted would have been a failure… So there is a part of me that thinks: that wasn't a very smart thing to do.

There was a sort of mismatch of the title – 'Reportage' – and its content that was not concerned with topicality. You know, the work didn't need to be topical to be there. Was there more continuity with the 'Independent Magazine'?

There was continuity I would say because a lot of the 'Independent Magazine's' coverage was timeless. Sometimes there were retrospectives, sometimes it was a photographer that had concentrated on a subject over a long period of time and it could have been published any time and it happened to be then. I suppose I never got my head round what the connotations of the word reportage were. I looked on it not necessarily being news related or witness related, but more the concept of photographers going out and engaging with the observable world and telling stories that had to be sustained through their visual journalism, primarily. That's how I defined reportage in my mind… God, we spent weeks trying to come up with a title. It was the first one we came up with and it sort of went round the houses. Either all the good ones had already been taken or they sounded ponderous. So it was back to square one to call it 'Reportage'. But that linked more to the black-and-white versus colour debate than it did to the subject area. Though I do think that a lot of the features were classically defined reportage features.

I was looking at an edition recently that contained a picture story about the English class system and of course these are the subjects you associate with the lineage of this sort of photography. Perhaps one of the things 'Reportage' may have been was a sort of history magazine.

I didn't have a historical mission. I really think it was this thing about feeling a little empty at the way things had gone. And I defined myself as a working picture editor with a certain kind of photography and a certain kind of photographer and I could see that disappearing and I just wanted to hold on to it. This seemed to be one way of holding onto it. I don't regret having done it and sometimes I look back and think: that wasn't bad. Then I look at some other things and think: that was awful.

How did you arrive at the frequency and the dimensions, the design?

The frequency is the easiest to answer because it was just a financial decision based on the printing costs. The design, the format and the paper quality were in discussion with Simon Estherson. Simon wanted a simple design and I agreed with that. We weren't seeking to break new ground in design terms, we were seeking to maintain and to sustain a tradition of visual journalism that I felt was under threat. I remember Alexander Chancellor saying to the team at the 'Independent Magazine', that he wanted to produce a magazine that was collectable and not disposed of at the end of the week, and I think to a certain extent we succeeded in the early days. That definitely was part of my mission statement, I wanted something that people would feel was worth collecting and keeping.

How about design. Picture editing is what you do obviously, but design is key isn't it? It certainly was then. How would you talk about 'Reportage's' design now?

I would say it's unchallenging but appropriate for the stories we ran. I like bold headlines. I like the use of red. The presentation is extremely classical. We spent a lot of time on captions. I got colleagues at 'The Independent' to help with captions and text editing and I learned a lot from them. The way it works with most colour magazines is that the picture desk provides the information and the sub editors write the captions. But I was always interested in captions.

How did you work with the designer?

That was quite fraught in the sense that Simon Estherson was incredibly busy all the time and we were only paying his costs, not any fee. So he was doing it out of the goodness of his heart. It was a question of slotting it in when you could and that was probably one reason why we made the design quite simple because we both knew that there wasn't going to be enough time available – not that I am apologising for the design because it holds up now. Simon would take it away and do it when he could... So it wasn't like working on a magazine where the picture editor and the art editor are there communicating daily. It was like producing a quarterly on a weekly deadline.

If you work with a designer on a mass production the parameters are set, aren't they? There's only so much artiness or risk-taking built into the system. But when it's a new magazine and you are working with a designer who is donating his time, he might want to innovate. Was their any conflict over this?

Not a conflict, really but at times it did concern me that it was looking too kind of beautiful or "aesthetically pleasing".

The late sixties and seventies was the beginning of the end of the picture essay. During the eighties this type of material was more likely to be found in books and big exhibitions. So here was an opportunity to do something unique: that is give this photography a new context.

You're right. The honest answer is that I was the wrong person to come up with that. I was steeped in a tradition that I liked and I still like.

It may be that no one would have done it anyway.

Maybe.

It was a brave thing to have done – without any criticism intended. To almost drag this photography out of being this ossified thing, found in museums, back on to the bookshelves. It's amazing that you didn't let the awesome challenge of that get in the way.

It never occurred to me that it could have gone in an entirely different direction and I suppose the short answer is that I didn't want it to. Maybe now I wouldn't want this extremely conventional design. The thinking behind it was: let the visual journalism speak, provide good text, not too much of it. It was a high-risk strategy because it meant the pictures had to be really good. I don't think they always were but there was a kind of consistency...

What was 'Reportage about'?

I would say it was about photography in its relationship to the observable world and that it was trying to present a perspective on the world through the eyes of talented observers – photographers, photojournalists.

So that's about reporting?

Reporting and observing; is there a difference? Yes, you can observe and not report. It was also about a hidden world (not subterranean), a world that is being often photographed but not being seen through photographs. It goes back to the 'Independent Magazine' which is why I am completely unapologetic about the stuff we published because it was in that sense a bit of a revelation. You were revealing, not so much stories that people didn't know but ways of telling stories about the world that people hadn't seen. In my view, a lot of these stories wouldn't have appeared in mainstream magazines, so in that sense it was doing a bit of a service to photography.

When you were at the 'Independent Magazine' it seemed to represent the last outpost of these values you talk about and you have built a reputation as a champion of these values. 'Reportage' was made sense of by the difference of mainstream magazines and it represented some comment on that.

It was revenge (laughs). Not quite revenge but a cry of pain to be honest. It sounds a bit adolescent, but it was a cry of pain about what I saw was unhappy in the world of photography. That was my response to what was going on. As you well know other people took totally other routes, rejecting photojournalism going into an art-based or conceptual world, taking photography into directions that were a bit behind your question earlier: that it was an opportunity to do something different, it could have gone in almost any direction if I had been interested – but I wasn't interested.

Looking back now it must strike you how much the internet has become the new space for reportage. Can you remember if this was an issue in the mid-nineties?

Not really, no. To be honest I had a pretty limited perspective. But, as I said, things happened really fast; I had a contract with Balding and Mansell and within weeks we just had to produce it. I probably didn't spend enough time thinking about its evolution as a creature. In terms of current practice, internet and so on, I don't think it was in any way relevant to what I was thinking.

Who was the reader of 'Reportage'?

That's interesting. I made this assumption, which was probably naïve, that the world of photography would contain default buyers – that you wouldn't have to persuade photographers. The people I was aiming at were much more non-professional in terms of photography. My prototypical reader was my GP who was a very keen amateur photographer. I had this reader profile: they were professional – they could be designers, architects, doctors, solicitors – people who had an interest in the world and were kind of motivated enough to look at photographs on a page. So they would probably like colour magazines when they were doing decent stories. I definitely wasn't aiming to be a niche magazine for people in the photography world – for I just assumed they would be interested anyway, if not as readers then as potential contributors. Which was an assumption that was proved wrong pretty rapidly. Some photographers did subscribe, but a lot didn't. I think at one point we did a readership survey and it was quite interesting the range of people that did subscribe. Without sounding pompous or pretentious, it was part of the mission statement to bring those stories to a wider (if small) audience than just the photography world.

(Colin refers to 'Reportage' Spring 95, issue 8. The magazine received £2000 from the Arts Council of England to commission a photographer, Caroline Penn and a writer Wendy Wallace, to produce a story about and to take pictures of Sikh women labouring in the country.)

That issue gave me great pleasure and it was one of the few times we really commissioned a story. The big drawback, when I look back, was that we weren't able to commission things; nearly all the stuff was stuff that had been shot already. This was much more like a traditional relationship between picture editor/editor and photographer and I think it works much better. We didn't do much of that. Maybe we managed two or three. The vast proportion of work – not unlike the 'Independent Magazine' – would come shot. It seemed to me that this is what magazines should have been doing in 1995. They weren't really interested in that kind of agenda. That was a classic piece of reportage, a writer and a photographer ... that kind of symbiotic relationship between two journalists. That to me is what good magazine journalism is about.

Did you feel it was a collective project? You and the photographers.

Yeah up to a point, partly because most of them were giving their work free (the second edition we paid very minimal page rate, £50). I did look on it as being collaborative rather than collective. It was mutually beneficial. I provided the vehicle, they provided the material and we both got something out of it.

How did you get on with advertising. Was another part of the mission to keep ads out of the editorial pages?

I wouldn't have rejected back page ads. Olympus [Optical UK] did some over four issues and Fuji did some over four issues. I wasn't proud in that sense. I would have taken ads, but again I was naïve and didn't know any thing about the advertising business. I tried pretty hard. But aside from these niche advertisers like Fuji and Olympus, nobody seemed to see the point of advertising with us.

Can you recall the circumstances of the collapse of the first version of 'Reportage'?

Adele, who was a publisher who was working for 'The Wire', basically just said: Look, you're going bust. She was monitoring the sales. It might have been the issue before the one before we folded. She said: It's had it. My first reaction was, I better write to all the subscribers. Then we sent out a lot of apologetic letters to subscribers saying, sorry, tried our best. If you want your money back then write. Most people were very good (and didn't ask for a refund). Quite a few people didn't lose that much. One or two people wanted to be paid back. I think I was quite exhausted by then. It wasn't that I was expecting it, but it wasn't quite the savage blow it might have been.

Where did 'Reportage' succeed and how and where did it fail and how?

It failed because it didn't continue. I suppose that's the obvious answer. I think it failed for some of the reasons you've touched on. It was reflecting an era that no longer seemed relevant to many people, it was part of a tradition that seemed to have come to a natural end. Maybe it was a sort of swansong for that era. It was kind of the end of the line for this approach to journalism.

It has migrated to books now.

Exactly. Books are great but I still like that organic side of magazines. Books are a bit … eternal. The failures were I suppose not to adjust to a more contemporary kind of publication that might have drawn in a wider circle. I was a bit stubborn in that I didn't want to compromise too much. Maybe we would have had a better chance of surviving if we had made some different design decisions, but then I wouldn't have been happy doing that. Objectively speaking, it was just a creature out of time. Successes? Over four years it managed to hang on to that idea that there are interesting, sometimes important stories being photographed by intelligent, perceptive photographers that ought to be seen a lot more regularly than they are, more or less around the time they were taken rather than in 20 years time when they might have a different kind of meaning. Just to keep this kind of work in a very small way in the pubic domain I think was a success. I won't make greater claims than that. I suppose on a personal level, it kept my sanity...

Yet its very existence seems to tell us something about the time.

Yeah. Just the fact that it came out was sufficient justification. I was very pleased that three or four stories (they were layouts) from 'The Independent' got into 'Things As They Are' [i], that was basically a history of magazines from the very beginning of World Press Photo. And they reproduced at least two stories from 'Reportage'. To me that was kind of pleasing. You know, in there among the 'New Yorker' and Time and so on. It's part of the record, and the history of magazine journalism. I think the story about camp S-21 went into the book. That is pleasing.

Did you feel you deserved more support?

I felt marginally disappointed that I worked so hard to get the natural catchment area for subscribers: photographers. What's crucial is that everybody at that time was moaning about the way photojournalism was fading away, and that lifestyle was dominant. As I said before, I decided, for whatever personal and professional reasons, to do something about it – because I had this windfall. Given that I did that – that was my contribution if you like, to try to answer these moans – therefore I did expect somehow that I would get a lot more subscriptions from people who were feeling that that world was disappearing. I had to work really hard, you know, to get subscribers and to get people to re-subscribe. I think I just felt slightly hurt that it was proving such hard work... But everyone says subscriptions-based magazines is hard work anyway.

'Reportage' has a sort of afterlife on the internet.

We put a lot of back numbers when we could. We put as much as we could of past editions. This is with my Dutch partner... We started to put new stories up almost immediately after the last print edition for about a year. They were kind of clumsily presented. We were working in the same way, talking to photographers, getting stories. Obviously putting them up in a different way, probably with a lot more pictures. But we both ran out of steam because it took up a lot of time, there was no money we were both doing other things, but it's up there now. It looks very old-fashioned compared with other photo sites because it hasn't been updated. I think it's quite interesting.

[i] Caujole, C. and Panzer, M. (2005). Things As They Are: Photojournalism in Context Since 1955. London: Chris Boot World Press Photo.

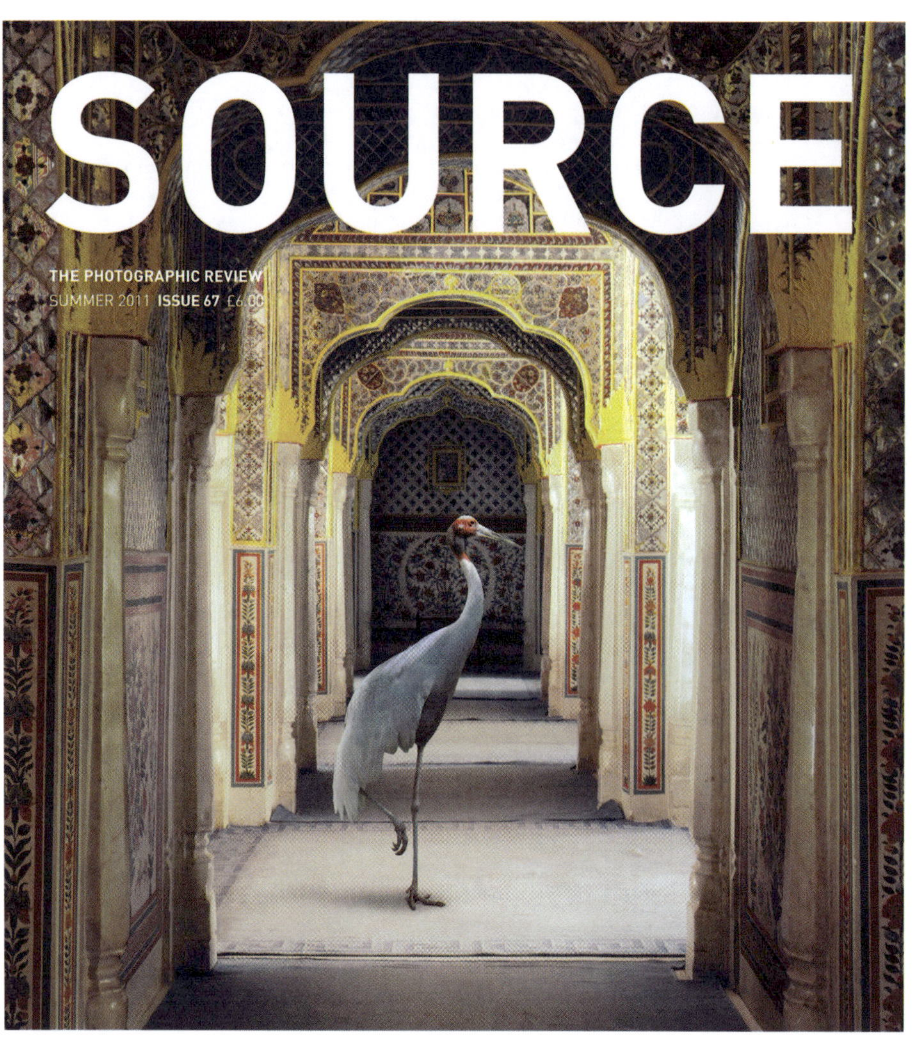
SOURCE
THE PHOTOGRAPHIC REVIEW
SUMMER 2011 ISSUE 67 £6.00

Richard West: *Source Photographic Review*

Founded in 1992, 'Source' grew out of a perceived need, among photographers in Northern Ireland, for a dedicated forum and platform. The editors are Richard West and John Duncan.

David Brittain: 'Source' is still in publication. Tell me the background.

Richard West: The magazine started in 1992 and the organization that published it, Photoworks North, was started the year before. To begin with it was a newsletter that was produced mainly to give publicity for other activities, things like workshops. They aspired to start a photography gallery, to allow people to meet up and exchange knowledge about things, and to be a focus for people interested in photography in Northern Ireland. Slowly, Photoworks North became less active and the publication it was producing became larger. It started to get a little bit of Arts Council funding and to establish distribution. The first two issues were free but soon it was available in newsagents and, because there wasn't anything else like it, it picked up a lot of readers in Ireland. I came along in 1997; up until that stage it had been run by my co-editor John Duncan, so I know more about what happened from that point. At that stage it was a strange mixture of a local magazine that was informed by a particular local interest – it reviewed very small exhibitions in Belfast – but it also had a wider network of connections. So, for example, John would know a photographer in France who would send some work, or someone would send work from elsewhere in Europe. The issues from around that period are A4 format, black and white, very classically produced. They are often a strange mixture: photograms, portraits, maybe a couple of reviews. The written content was less important than the photographic work, maybe it would contextualise some of it. After I started working on it the written content – specifically a more defined reviews section – started to grow. We already had international distribution by that stage but over the years, from 1998, we began to refine our ideas about what constituency we were dealing with: mainly the UK and Ireland. Since then the magazine has got bigger, a large part of it is now given over to exhibition reviews, book reviews and a news section. We have a much clearer idea of our connection to the UK and Ireland.

When 'Source' became a magazine what could people buy in Northern Ireland to read about photography?

I don't think you could buy anything except the camera magazines and the 'British Journal of Photography' probably. It's interesting to extend the question and ask: who were the people who wanted to produce this magazine? Who were the people who started Photoworks North? They were people who had a specific interest – maybe they had done a photography degree in Britain (there were no photography degrees in Ireland at that stage) and came back with the flaming torch of we-want-to-treat-photography-as-a-special-thing. They might say "It can be done in this way, with an emphasis on authorship, this is the kind of work we are interested in". It was a bit like the missionary zeal that you see in the 1970s in 'Creative Camera'. There were precedents: there had been issues of 'Creative Camera' that had been dedicated to Northern Ireland in the eighties and there were people who had produced significant work already, like Victor Sloan. There had been exhibitions that had identified some people: Willie Doherty, Paul Seawright, Anthony Haughey. Paul Seawright was listed as the editor of the first issue of the magazine. So these were the people who were carrying the torch. Consider this gang, they were not informed by what they could buy in newsagents but by their connection to a bigger discussion that was based around things like 'Creative Camera' and exhibitions...

The missionary zeal you mention was probably missing in most British institutions that supported photography by the mid-nineties.

It is partly to do with who I am and who John is. My background is in philosophy. So I was coming to photography fresh-faced. John studied photography at Glasgow School of Art and Newport, so he identified with a documentary tradition but also an idea of fine art photography. He was aware of the idea of theory as this thing that people were slightly afraid of and that it was requisite, but slightly in conflict with, the authored photography of the documentary tradition. We were aware of this conflict but didn't feel inhibited by it. Our enthusiasm was of a person who takes photographs and still has an interest in discovering other people who are doing the same thing. I remember conversations in the late nineties when we were comparing ourselves to 'Creative Camera'. We saw ourselves very much on the edge, beneath everyone's notice and we didn't feel an entitlement to address some things, as if the definitive statements had already been made elsewhere. It's interesting looking back on it; we're talking about arguments about theory and about authored photography from the eighties and the nineties but really, of course, what was happening at that time was Gursky and all these big photography exhibitions. In a way this was the realization of everyone's ambitions –the success of photography in the art market – and we felt the opportunity that was there: we now had this massive explosion of material for a magazine to comment on and discuss. A lot of people were suddenly interested in photography. You may still feel you're sniping from the sidelines, which has always been the case with photography – but now there are people who represent what you are interested in, in the big institutions and big publishers.

My experience at Creative Camera" taught me that the memories of the fight for photography, so to speak, were very fresh.

Obviously we inherited a certain version of that. I also should say that I made a conscious effort – the way you did – to put on the mantle of that tradition by finding out about it. I would go and listen to the photography interviews in the oral history archive at the British Library (they're a great way of hearing from the horse's mouth). Then I started doing interviews myself and I would hear a lot of these stories from these old photography people simply by having the opportunity to sit down and talk to them. It's interesting the way you describe it, because it is true that this tradition is powerful... but the other thing that happens in the 1990s is new people come along that don't know anything about this and don't care ...

One of our roles, as I saw it, was to be first to show stuff to the community and this was an essential niche for the magazine. But gradually it became that this new material, the latest Friedlander *images say, was coming out of other places and we weren't the first. We had lost that role. 'Source' had a big commitment to new stuff and that was commendable in contrast to other magazines ... so there was a need to key in with a moment?*

Actually, I think this is something different about our perspectives; between being deeply embedded in this world in London and being in Belfast. Essentially our rationale is not about finding the new thing because the thing that we are most interested in finding, is not only not new – it's unknown.

I should have said new/unknown because at one point they were the same.

In the Friedlander case that's not true. It's new but not unknown as it has already been valorized by the Museum of Modern art.

New to the community if you like ...

But that's one difference between 'Creative Camera' and 'Source'. The 1970 'Creative Camera' is bringing the message from across the sea; 'Source' is bringing the message from the back woods where a woman is making photographs you've never seen before... of goldfish. That, in caricature, is the difference. The principle of 'Source' is not to find the next big thing but to find what is beneath anyone's notice. We are the people who go into the woods to find it. Even by the year 2000 the photography institutions in the country – this is just based on what other people say – were not open to the punter that has no reputation. And so we felt, and still do, that we're on a similar level to these people who have no status. So we have gone to out-of-the-way arts centres and anyone can come along and show us their work and they will be treated in the same way as the famous person. Whereas, if you are running the Photographers' Gallery, you spend most of your life trying to avoid these people who are coming in and pestering you for an exhibition.

Let's say you've got a dozen of these submissions, how do you decide which are the best?

John acts as the initial filter for this – maybe he has met someone who has shown him the pictures, or he encourages them and they send some work. Maybe we have ten or 15 pieces of work that we are considering for one issue and we are going to publish three of them. We edit them on the table. I say, Why do you like this picture?, we discuss them and make a decision.

What bearing on your decision about content has the identity of the magazine, its identity as you want it to appear to readers?

We are not trying to identify the magazine through the work we publish, it's the other way round. We have to feel that we are excited, or there is something valuable in publishing whatever it is we are going to publish.

Does it in some curious way reflect its roots?

Yes it does. My description of the way we find work is an assertion that we are conscientious, it's a declaration of our earnestness, our willingness to meet people on a level playing field and I think that's partly to do with the idea of being slightly away from the centre.... What are the key issues for a photography magazine in the past 30 years? You can tell that story in lots of different ways. There are things we haven't mentioned, like for example computers. When I started, we were receiving medium format transparencies and now everything comes through email. Things are far easier to find out about. There's been an absolute explosion of photographic publishers in the last ten years. In terms of the institutional history we're talking about, I think it's important to be able to step back from and be empowered by the history of these organizations. You don't want to get stuck, like a mammoth in a tar pit, worrying about whether or not to change the names of the two galleries at the Photographers' Gallery …

I agree that isn't key to what a photography magazine is for but I think the relationship between the community and the institutions that serve it is some kind of litmus about the state of what you might call photography. And there is a new, cooler relationship as a result of the professionalizing of the nineties.

There is no entitlement to this tradition. You were the person that was part of the gang and read the 'Open Eye' magazine, then, come 2010 you feel annoyed that Hans-Peter Feldmann appears in 'Frieze', and not in a photography magazine; you feel that that's *our* photography, it's not *their* photography. It should be the other way round, the excitement of photography is that it belongs to everyone, and now it is in a much broader cultural context.

What is your model for 'Source'?

If we're talking about magazines the key magazine for 'Source' is probably the 'Times Literary Supplement' in terms of … the idea of a kind of public conversation. A large part of 'Source' is given over to reviews and the purpose of the reviews is to allow someone to think seriously about an exhibition or a book for 900 words. Going back to the topic of what has changed, the photography world is more diverse: recycling photographic archives, the growth in photographic history and theory books, people in literature departments writing about photography… And these are things that offer new opportunities. W.G. Sebald is an interesting example. We reviewed 'Austerlitz' when it came out and I remember when we reviewed it thinking: It's a small detail in the magazine but we're making a point by the emphasis we're putting on it.

There are many different ways to signal change – you change design, etc. Such changes happen at all levels among all magazines and always have done. When you do something unusual such as reviewing a Sebald novel you signal change by contesting the identity of the magazine – something unthinkable in a mainstream title.

There are different reasons to be interested in photography. One is that there is a small group of people who are trying to use it as a creative art form. Another is that it infuses the world. In the last 10 years those two things have come together slightly. So W.G. Sebald is an interesting case; a novelist that is also asking you to think about anonymous photographs (embedded into his text, forming a complementary narrative) that would normally be beneath anyone's notice. You are looking at pictures (that are generally very ordinary looking) while at the same time Sebald demonstrates the most heightened idea of what photographic expression could achieve.

Yet you have a very conservative role, which is to promote an art of photography…

I bridle at the word promote.

Perhaps you don't promote it, but you give it a particular space, get intelligent writers to talk about it, and you make reputations, and that's what I did. That's a role that started with Stieglitz.

You're asking: Why do a photography magazine?

Perhaps.

I am bridling at the word promote because I think that another key component of being the type of magazine I am talking about is to be independent. We have to be able to annoy everybody. Everyone who writes for the magazine needs to be able to say of the book that they are reviewing – no matter how shiny it is – or the exhibition they are reviewing – no matter how prestigious it is – that they think it's rubbish. A recurrent question at the magazine is: if photography ceased to be interesting would we stop doing it? We don't owe an allegiance to photography. We do a photography magazine because we continue to be interested by the things it throws up ...

What about: 'What is photography?'

What is photography? In our case photography is an opportunity to talk about lots of different things, because they are touched by photography, and an opportunity to talk about things that are particular to photography, like the way it records things, the strange fluctuating role it has of being both caused by the thing it represents and being apparently blank and open to being read in any way we want. It's a tool for people to use as a creative means in myriad different ways, and it's something that has been involved in human history; it's a key component of contemporary media, and lots of other things besides. It's a pretext for doing interesting stuff.

There are many types of photography magazine and you have described yours, based on the review format of the 'TLS'. But it strikes me that every photography magazine belongs to "the field". This is different from somehow deciding you will have a photographic perspective. Which is what you seem to be describing. One of the things that gives 'Source' its photographic perspective is that it displays all the signs of what is recognized to be a good photography magazine. What I am saying is that the photographic context is transcendent of editorial agendas.

There's kind of a closed system version of photography and an open system version of photography. The closed version is for people who are standing in the castle trying to prevent anyone from coming inside the battlements and they're saying: "Everything in the corral is photography". And the open system is: Everything you can see is possibly within your ambit; and that's the version we're working with. In practice the people bringing us portfolios are in a certain tradition, they're all in the UK and Ireland so they have a certain perspective themselves, but despite that there is still a very wide range of people doing a wide range of things… It needn't be a limiting thing. The opportunity for someone to do something as a photographer is almost unlimited.

What I think you do is to take discussions you find around you in different places – in the 'TLS' *for instance – and bring them into your photographic context. Why is it a photographic context? It may be that this is what defines a photography magazine – something that nurtures reputations, creates rankings based on ideas of good and bad and so on.*

Essentially we have a more sympathetic context than I think you were in. The most important thing is producing something for the readership, not any particular vested interests. I think we are quite fortunate in that we benefit from being in Belfast because none of the photography institutions has any power over us. It doesn't matter to us what the Photographers' Gallery thinks of us.

You have a board?

We have a board. The people on the board are a mixture of artists, photographers, a couple of writers. We have dealings with two arts councils – one in Dublin and one in Belfast. And the issue there that is tricky, in terms of how their interests coincide with our interests, is to do with the constituency we are serving, because obviously we cover stuff that is outside of the constituencies of those two arts councils. So the Arts Council of Northern Ireland is concerned with supporting arts in Northern Ireland. Other than that their concerns are to do with things like keeping accurate finances and things like that. They don't have a predetermined idea of what a photography magazine should be…

I am asking, rhetorically I suppose, if a photography magazine can exist outside of the pressures of the "business"?

Maybe it is impossible to do it in London. It does come back round to the fact that we are in Belfast. It manifests itself in every aspect of the magazine. We are as interested in what happens in the Northern Gallery of Contemporary Art, that do a lot of photography exhibitions, as we are in the Photographers' Gallery… As far as we can see being in Belfast gives you a great perspective to give all these institutions across the country parity.

Do you think 'Source' advances an agenda for change?

Well, yes there is a sort of ethic to do with how work is treated and to do with respect due to people who are producing work.

That is more like a description of your values. Is there also a catalyst function?

The catalyst function is probably to do with the things we find stimulating, so for instance the discussion we had about Sebald. It's not that we had a mission to generate this change but I think you see this stuff bubbling up and you want to find other books like this, review them so that this will provoke discussion.

Even though you're in Belfast and nobody is pressurizing you, there is this history that – even if you do not acknowledge its influence – you and your contributors are alluding to, arguing with, ignoring it deliberately and so on. You have no control over that.

I can see that this photographic history – that is 30 years of people arguing about photography – could be debilitating, because it is fractious and it is easy to get bogged down in…

I am saying that you can't escape.

Maybe, but it doesn't have to be a drag.

No, but much is prescribed. The book, 'Challenging Art: Artforum (1962-1974)' was sort of snapshot of a bigger process that was happening all round the world (the rejection of Greenbergian aesthetics and the rise of postmodernism). Exactly the same thing happened at 'Creative Camera' in 1980 after the title became a recipient of Arts Council funding, everybody seemed to divide into modernists and postmodernists. That was symbolic of a change that happened not just locally, but internationally. This says that there is a larger, inscribed history here to the world you work within. You're right that is doesn't have to be a drag, but it's there.

Of course, yeah. It's probably invisible to a degree, but we are in a bigger context. And the photography world is just a bit of that.

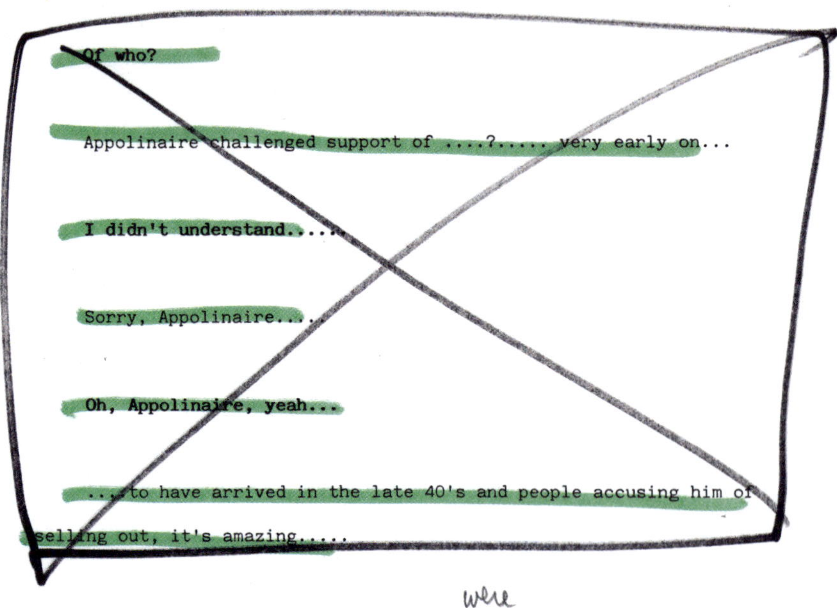

\- 7 -

Of who?

Appolinaire challenged support of ....?..... very early on...

I didn't understand.....

Sorry, Appolinaire.....

Oh, Appolinaire, yeah...

.....to have arrived in the late 40's and people accusing him of selling out, it's amazing.....

What follows is the transcript of the previous text after the interviewer, David Brittain, had made initial changes to clarify his questions. The interviewee, Richard West, is yet to correct the raw text for mistakes and make the changes he feels are needed to help clarify his responses. The final format emerged over several months only after both parties made further additions and cuts, and once each was satisfied with his respective contribution.

Richard West and David Brittain in conversation
7 June 2010 Belfast

I hope we can talk about the specialism of the photography magazine. 'Source' is the only title to be included in this project that is still being published. Tell me the background.

Yes, from 98 we began to refine our ideas about what constituency we were dealing with: mainly the UK and Ireland. Since then the magazine has grown, a large part of the magazine is now given over to exhibition reviews, book reviews and a news section. We have a much clearer idea of our connection to the UK and Ireland.

When 'Source' became a magazine what could people buy in NI to read about photography?

I don't think you could buy anything except the camera magazines and the 'BJP' probably. It's interesting to extend the question and ask: who are the people who wanted to produce this magazine? Who are the people who started Photoworks North? They are people who had a specific interest – maybe they did a photography degree in the uk (there were no photography degrees in Ireland at that stage) and they have come back with the flaming torch of we-want-to-treat-photography-as-a-special-thing. It can be done in this way with an emphasis on authorship and this is the kind of work we are interested in. It's a bit like the missionary zeal that you see in the 1970s in 'Creative Camera'. There were precedents: there had been an issue of 'Creative Camera' that had been dedicated to Northern Ireland in the 80s and there were people who produced significant work for that like Victor Sloan. There have been exhibitions that identified some people who have some history, people like Willie Doherty, Paul Seawright, Anthony Haughey, these people. Paul Seawright was listed as the editor of the first magazine. So these are the people who are carrying the torch. Asking about distribution, that gang of people are not informed by what they can buy in newsagents but by their connection to a bigger discussion that is based around things like 'Creative Camera' and exhibitions…

The missionary zeal you mention was probably missing in most British institutions that supported photography by the mid 90s. When I began editing 'Creative Camera' in 1991 I felt that not only had the missionary zeal been supplanted, it had been supplanted by another type of missionary zeal based on attacking the perceived modernism of the old 'Creative Camera'. And somehow now that zeal was fading and we were in a holding pattern awaiting the next thing. So that's a very contrasting situation.

It is partly to do with who I am and who John is. My background is in philosophy. So I was coming to photography fresh-faced. John studied photography at Glasgow and then Newport, so he had a documentary tradition but also an idea of fine art photography. He was aware of the idea of theory as this thing that people were slightly afraid of and that it was requisite but slightly in conflict with the authored photography of the documentary tradition. We were aware of this conflict but didn't feel inhibited by it because the enthusiasm of a person who takes photographs and the interest in discovering other people who do that is still there.

I wonder if that enthusiasm would have been found anywhere else in Britain at the time.

We saw ourselves as being on the periphery of things. I remember conversations in the late 90s when we were comparing ourselves to 'Creative Camera'. We saw ourselves very much on the edge, beneath everyone's notice and we didn't feel an entitlement to address things as if the definitive statements had been made elsewhere about these things. It's interesting looking back on it; I mean we're talking about arguments about theory and about authored photography from the 80s and the 90s and that was the background – but really of course what was happening at that time was Gursky and all these big photography exhibitions and now these big celebrity photographers were eclipsing all this stuff that had happened in the past. In a way it was the realization of everyone's ambitions for 20 years and part of the opportunity that was there – even if we felt we were small voices – was that we now had this massive explosion of material for a magazine to comment on and discuss. So we felt there was a possibility. People were suddenly interested in photography. You may still feel you're sniping from the sidelines, which has always been the case with photography – but now there are people who represent what you are interested in, in the big institutions and producing big books.

Yeah, I was more aware of continuity of readership. I would meet readers who were older than me who could talk about knowing Bill Jay or Peter Turner; this is the late 60s early 70s. So there was an oppressive sense of a tail to this beast that stretched way back. Some of these people had lived through things that I only knew from history or never knew. They'd watched the magazine change, may have stopped subscribing at some stage because, say, the editorship of Susan Butler was annoying to them, and had maybe gone back again. So there was very much a sense of a community that was already there, installed and wiser than me when I arrived in 1991. I was inhibited by that yet saw something different was happening, the arrival of people with no memory of all this. I was in two minds about this: on the one hand this could be liberating, on the other hand it was part of the magazine's job to remember …

How did that manifest itself?

I think by the articles. There were even articles commenting on the fact that photography only reached this privileged place after a lot of negotiation – maybe you will find these comments in reviews. That is in contrast to your experience.

Obviously we inherited a certain version of that. I also should say that I made a conscious effort – the way you did – to kind of put on the mantle of that tradition by finding out about it. I would go and listen to the interviews in the oral history archive at the British Library; they're a great way of hearing from the horse's mouth ... And people like Chris Boot actually who has a path through this and is still publishing photography books. Then I started doing these interviews myself so when I would do an interview for the magazine – which wasn't that often – and I would hear a lot of these stories from these people simply by having the opportunity to sit down and talk to them ... It's interesting the way you describe it because it is true that this tradition is powerful because people have been arguing about things for a while, and they can claim things as giving them value, but the other thing that happens in the 1990s is new people come along that don't know anything about this and don't care ...

To reiterate what you said: my university was the 'Amateur Photographer' where I worked for about five years from 1980 and where I met so many people and absorbed all this history. I had no idea that there was a support structure for photography, that there were so many personal conflicts and troubles... I discovered that an artist such as Victor Burgin, who was working against the modernist tradition using text and image, and a photojournalist who was absolutely for it, are both equal within this system and are able to claim money to support their practice. These anomalies fascinated me as perhaps being non-existent outside of this weird world and obviously much was learnt from review books .... It was from that position that I began to edit 'Creative Camera' – as an outsider, a total voyeur because I didn't feel that was my life or my story. But I understood the meaning of the stories because I'd heard them and knew the context. Another change was the market, the secondary market – there was suddenly this idea of the "classic period" of photography; there was "Modernist photography" and all this stuff that was junk in the 70s was suddenly massively valuable. That had an effect on what you were writing.

I think the only expression of that was the scarcity of books from pre-1970... Something else interesting happened. That is over the last 10 years a lot of (photojournalistic) material started to be rediscovered; there have been exhibitions about the magazine press; I must have commissioned reviews of four or five books about the history of press photography (for instance, 'Kiosk') and suddenly Rodchenko and all these people come back into circulation …

Another thing that was notable was – and this became a real challenge for me – that one of our roles, as I saw it, was to be first to show stuff to the community and this was an essential niche for the magazine. But gradually it became that this new material, the latest Friedlander images say, was coming out of other places and we weren't the first. We had lost that role. 'Source' had a big commitment to new stuff and that was commendable in contrast to other magazines … so there was a need to key in with a moment?

Actually it's not true. It's interesting that you say that and I think it's something different about our perspectives between being deeply embedded in this world in London and being in Belfast. Essentially our rationale is not about finding the new thing because the thing that we are most interested in finding, is not only not new – it's unknown.

I should have said new/unknown because at one point they were the same.

In the Friedlander case that's not true. It's unknown but not new as it has already been valorized by the Museum of Modern art.

New to the community if you like …

But that's one difference between 'Creative Camera' and 'Source'. The 1970 'Creative Camera' is bringing the message from across the sea; 'Source' is bringing the message from the back wood where the woman is making photographs you've never seen before of goldfish. That's in caricature, the difference. The principle of 'Source' is not to find the next big thing but to find what is beneath everyone's notice.

I think that was what I was trying to do too, to find the obscure, but also to find the discussion for the obscure. Or sometimes the other way round: you'd find the discussion then have to find the images.

Without wanting to be pedantic, it's not the obscurity, it's to do with how these things are institutionally supported. So the point about the woman in the back woods is not what she's doing is obscure so much as the fact that no one else is going to pay attention to it. We are the people who go into the woods to find it. Even by the year 2000 the photography institutions in the country – this is just based on what other people say – are not interested in going and finding or being open to some punter that has no reputation. And so we felt – still do to an extent – that we're on a similar level to these people who have no status. So we have traditionally gone to out-of-the-way arts centres and anyone can come along as see us and they will be treated in the same way as the famous person. Whereas if you are running the Photographers' Gallery you spend most of your life trying to avoid these people who are coming in and pestering you for an exhibition.

Let's say you've got a dozen of these submissions, how do you decide which are the best of that dozen?

We put it on the table and we look at it a lot. Well actually it doesn't really work like that. John acts as the initial filter for this – maybe he has met someone who has showed him the pictures or he encourages them and they send some work so maybe we have ten of 15 pieces of work that we are considering for one issue and we are going to publish three of them. We edit them on the table; I say, why do you like this picture? And he says well, you say it's about death but if you look carefully the woman's smiling (I am imaging a conversation). If you put up pictures and you discover that you like them – which often happens quite quickly – and a couple of weeks later you still like them then that's something you will probably stick with.

What bearing on your decision has the identity of the magazine, its identity as you want it to appear to readers?

That's interesting ... it's not that we are trying to present a version of the magazine by the work we publish, it's the other way round. We may think: are we getting lazy here? ... We have to feel that we are excited or there is something valuable in publishing whatever it is we are going to publish.

Does it in some curious way reflect its roots?

Yes it does. In what I have described about the way we go and find work I am giving an assertion that we are conscientious and it's a declaration of our earnestness, our willingness to meet people on a level playing ground and I think that's partly to do with the idea of being slightly away from the centre.

That sentiment seems to belong to the "golden age" of photography prior to a kind of professionalization of institutions ... The sense that everybody owned the resource – say it was a gallery and the door was open for users – prevailed for a number of years but was suddenly over. There was some pressure too to professionalise 'Creative Camera.'

What do you mean by professionalise?

To professionalise is to have higher production values, better design – to be less polyphonic and to become more corporate in some ways. To sort of vanish behind some façade. I saw that happen at the Photographers' Gallery – the photographers' with a possessive meant it belonged to photographers. Gradually the photographers felt they had no control or investment and a distancing was achieved through how the gallery was painted, the design, architecture, all sorts of managerial devices and signs. And you can find the equivalent in the magazines. So by contrast you guys sound down and dirty and you're talking to people like you that way people in institutions used to speak to photographers. That's my point.

You asked: What are the key things for a photography magazine in the past thirty years? You can tell that story in lots of different ways. There are things we haven't mentioned, like for example computers, that means by the time I came along at 'Source' it was possible to do everything myself because it is so easy with the internet and because, in the old days when I started, we were receiving medium format transparencies and now everything comes through email. Things are far easier to find out about. There's been an absolute explosion of photographic publishers in the last 10 years. And the institutional history we're talking about – finding out how long these organisations have been going, how long these people have been involved, all the arguments – I think the real trick is to be able to step back from that to a certain extent and both be empowered by that, the history of these organizations, but also not to be stuck like a mammoth in a tarpit worrying in some atavistic anxiety about whether or not to change the names of the two galleries at the Photographers' Gallery …

I agree that isn't key to what a photography magazine is for but I think the relationship between the community and the institutions that serve it is some kind of litmus about the state of what you might call photography. And there is a new, cooler relationship. People who supported these little magazines – Open Eye in Liverpool had its own little magazine – saw them as being empowering, as a lobbying tool even.

The negative side of that is when, ten years later, you end up with this feeling of entitlement to this tradition. So you are the person that was part of the gang and read the 'Open Eye magazine' and then come 2010 you feel annoyed that Hans-Peter Feldman appears in 'Frieze', and doesn't appear in a photography magazine – you feel that that's OUR PHOTOGRAPHY, it's not their photography. Whereas I think it should always be the other way round where the excitement of photography is that it belongs to everyone and the fact that people had to carve out this narrow band version of photography in the past, to claim it as interesting shouldn't limit the fact that now it is interesting in a much broader cultural context.

Something you confirm is my instinct that these magazines are not really magazines, or are anti-magazines (mainstream titles are of course very conservative, predictable, they give people what they want and are cyclical – seasonal). These respond to changes differently.

If we're talking about magazines the key magazine for 'Source' is probably the 'TLS' in terms of ... the idea of a kind of public conversation. So a large part of 'Source' is given over to reviews and the purpose of the reviews is to create or foster an audience for people who are interested in someone sitting down and thinking seriously about an exhibition or a book for 900 words. And that's what the 'TLS' does and that's the model. There is no other photography magazine that has done that – have a substantial review content.

The 'Creative Camera' of the 80s, of Susan Butler or Mark Holborn was very review heavy. I'd like to return to the idea of the magazine that changes. I have worked on a few mainstream magazines that just go round and round a track with the seasons. Magazines should do that though. I felt that 'Creative Camera' had to keep changing to reflect the changes in the world around it. That makes an unusual magazine. Do you feel you are doing that?

I think that 'Source' and other magazines like ours are inevitably going to change more because we don't publish that many issues, we're not a large organisation ... 'Source' has 88 pages and comes out four times a year and has two people involved and 20 contributors. So not much has to change for these people to have a considerable impact on the magazine. Or a significant event like the Tate starting to show photography or books coming out that can change the general complexion of things. I think in that sense we are reactive, we want to be both responsive to what's out there but also we, in a way, serve a function for our readership by recognising a certain idea of what the important thing is and making sure we find out about it and get the right person to write about it; that's a basic function of the magazine and we have to do that well.

Going back to the topic of what has changed, there are so many projects today – like these people that are recycling photographic archives to make exhibitions or the growth in photographic history or theory books, people in literature departments – writing about photography, those are things that offer new opportunities. WG Sebald is an interesting character, we reviewed 'Austerlitz' – and there wouldn't have been the opportunity to do that in the 1990s – and I remember when we reviewed that thinking: It's a small detail in the magazine but we're making a point by the emphasis we're putting on it.

That example is close to what I am trying to get at about these magazines not behaving like normal magazines. There are many different ways to signal change – you change design. Or you remove the news because you lack resources to do that. Those changes happen at all levels among all magazines and always have done. When you do something unusual such as reviewing a Sebald novel YOU SIGNAL THAT PHOTOGRAPHY IS CHANGING AND THAT THIS HAS CHANGED ONE OF ITS MAGAZINES IRREVOCABLY.

You are saying something has changed but that it can mean different things; it might reflect either the fact that you were first to notice it or that you noticed that someone else saw its significance.

A zoologist can have the same discussion about the ecosphere by looking at the ant or looking at the forest. So, for example, design. The magazine has been thoroughly redesigned two or three times since I have been here and the conversations around that have been very interesting. We go and get a heap of different magazines, put them down and talk about what we like from the different magazines. The question of a sea change – to coin a cliché – in photography, I think there have been a number of these. From my own point of view I have always been interested in a broad conception of photography and a part of the ethos of the magazine has been this authored photography, art photography but also not authored photography, photography as cultural phenomenon and I think a reason to be interested in photography is that you both represent a small group of people who are trying to use this as a creative art form but you are also interested in it because it infuses the world and in the last ten years those two things have come together slightly. So WG Sebald is an interesting case as somebody who is an author and he is asking you to think about anonymous photographs that would normally be beneath anyone's notice in this highly aestheticised context. So you are both looking at pictures that are the dross of junk shops – something that would never be worthy of conversation – at the same time it's the most heightened idea of what photographic expression could achieve.

I understand that. Yet you have a very conservative role which is to continually promote the art of photography...

I bridle at the word promote.

In context you do because many people do and it's certainly what we used to do. Perhaps you don't promote it but you give it a particular space, get intelligent writers to talk about it, and you make reputations, and that's what I did. That's a role that started with Stieglitz. For that staple role we got money from the

Arts Council. If we had stopped doing this then we would have had to have promoted something else – theoretical writing. Maybe the question is: to what degree does that advocacy role compromise you? Wouldn't it have been more interesting to talk about Sebald not from a photography point of view?

You're asking why do a photography magazine.

Yes.

I am bridling at the word promote because I think that another key component of being the type of magazine I am talking about ... is that we are not actually promoting. It is essential for us to be independent. ... We have to be able to annoy everybody. Everyone who writes for the magazine needs to be able to say of the book that are reviewing – no matter how shiny it is – or the exhibition they are reviewing – no matter how prestigious it is – that it is by no means so important to any photography constituency that I should say it's good when I think it's rubbish. A recurrent question at the magazine is: if photography ceased to be interesting would we stop doing it? And we don't owe an allegiance to photography. We do a photography magazine because we continue to be interested by the things it throws up .. Why photography?

What about: what is photography?

What is photography? In our case photography is an opportunity to talk about lots of different things that are touched by photography and an opportunity to talk about things that are particular to photography like the way it records things, the strange fluctuating role it has of being both caused by the thing it represents and being apparently blank and open to being read in any way we want. It's a tool for people to use as a creative means in myriad different ways, it's something that has been involved in human history, it's representable of human history; it's the means by which the media works and lots of other things besides. It's a pretext.

You say you were not promoting practices but I was at 'Creative Camera' – even if just by virtue of the fact that we received public funding on that basis. The practices we promoted were increasingly academic ones: photographers had MAs, writers were lecturers and so on. Increasingly the magazine became an adjunct of academia and I felt that I had no control over the context of this. I don't think we feel any of that. That's because Discussion refers to academia

You mentioned that the model for 'Source' was the 'TLS'. Well, if I'd had the choice

I would rather have edited the 'TLS' than a photography magazine because it has no advocacy agenda.

Well that goes to show what you think a photography magazine can be. Because I think a photography magazine can be anything.

Providing it's not in receipt of public funding that determines that it must be an advocate for certain photographic practices.

Let me answer that provocation. There are two bits to that. The first part is what is a photography magazine and I have tried to describe that as being equivalent to what the 'TLS' is doing. What I have tried to describe is that photography is the pretext for writing about interesting stuff – and that can be anything and I think in many senses that is the same thing the 'TLS' does. It obviously takes a different form. And the public funding thing, obviously that isn't true in the case of the 'TLS'.

There are many types of photography magazine and you have described yours, based on the review format of the 'TLS'. But it strikes me that every photography magazine shares a concern with "the field". This is different from somehow deciding you will have a photographic perspective. Which is what you seem to be describing. One of the things that gives 'Source' its photographic perspective is that it displays all the signs of a good photography magazine – it's a part of the community, it displays good design, has readers or funders that expect the magazine to favour photography as an autonomous art. What I am saying is that the photographic context is transcendent of editorial control.

There's a kind of a closed system version of photography and an open system version of photography. The closed version is for people who are standing in the castle trying to prevent anyone from coming inside the battlements and they're saying everything in the corral is photography. And the open system is everything you can see is possibly within your ambit; and that's the version we're working on. You're saying the photographic perspective is authored photography, it's articles about photography with a certain context. Surely that is in someway limited. I'm saying I have an open universe idea of what a photography magazine can cover: how can I possibly say that? In practice because, it may be that all these people bringing us portfolios are in a certain tradition, they're all in the UK and Ireland so they have a certain perspective themselves, but despite that there is still a very wide range of people doing a wide range of things... That needn't be a limiting thing. The opportunity for someone to do something as an authored photographer is almost unlimited. The articles have been about ... anything.

I think I was being as much of a collagist as you. That's what I think you do: take discussions you find around you in different places – in the 'TLS' for instance – and bring them into your photographic context. Why is it a photographic context? It may be that this is what defines a photography magazine – something that nurtures reputations, creates rankings based on ideas of good and bad and so on. Is the need to fulfill this advocacy function so compelling that no editor of a photography magazine can break the mould?

A different version of what the magazine would be would be a division between a polemical magazine and one that is more interested in reflecting the community. The polemical magazine always has a bit of fight (I suppose the tabloid in a way is polemically driven by a certain outraged morality). It think there's always a bit of an element of that. I really enjoy 'Private Eye' for example which has its own polemical standpoint and there is the dynamism the reader gets from taking a confrontational attitude – like the news reporting in 'Source'. You want to be able to stoke things up a bit. I think the magazine can contain different editorial approaches. You open it and there's a reporter saying: these guys are pathetic, they said they were going to build this gallery … but it's all hot air. OK? And the people reading that say: Alright I'm part of this gang, this gallery was supposed to be for me and I'm glad they've said that. You turn over the pages and now you've got eight or ten pages of some people in some gun club. Your relationship, as an editor, to that body of work is different from your relationship to the gallery and the news reporter. Your approach is one of receptiveness – that that person has come and shown you their work – and critical openness to allow you to look at it and try to understand it as completely as possible and then re-present it for the benefit of somebody who wants to look… Going back to your question of how you want to position a magazine, and how we see ourselves on the same level as these photographers, is that we don't have any polemical mission and we attempt to exclude it by the work we publish. We just want it to be good. Of course we have our own standpoint but we are not interested in our own standpoint – we're interested in giving space and presenting photographs well. If it turns out that all of the most interesting things are photojournalism in the next five years, and everyone says, oh God they're mad keen on photojournalism, then so be it! But it's not to do with the argument we want to make in terms of photography.

In contrast, I was under intense scrutiny at 'Creative Camera' because for the 48 or 49 per cent of our turnover that they supplied in grant funding the Arts Council demanded transparency. So that's a board they approved of, it's reports and so on and in our dealings there always had been a sense that let's say some people were being more favoured (by publication) than others. So the funding world reflected the struggles for representation in the boarder world of photography. The role I assumed historically was as a gatekeeper, someone who was seen by some to be tremendously generous to others while others saw me as an enemy of various types of photography. My questions come out of my conviction that 'Creative Camera' would have been a better magazine if I had stopped promoting reputations. And if possible to remove the title from the historical framework that lent it its photographic context. I think that was the problem Geoff Batchen encountered when he began editing 'Photofile' in the mid-80s. Can I ask about the funding climate you operate within.

Essentially we have a more sympathetic context; I can image the situation you were in. It becomes a horrific political job to try to maintain what is important – and the most important thing is producing something for the readership, not any of the vested interests. I think we are quite fortunate in that. We benefit a lot from being in Belfast because none of the institutions (that fund us?) has any power over us. We're not beholden to any photography organization... It doesn't matter to us what the Photographers' Gallery thinks of us.

You have a board?

We have a board. The people on the board are mostly artists, a couple of writers. They have no particular investment in the photography world. We have dealings with two arts councils – one in Dublin and one in Belfast. And the issue there that is tricky in terms of how their interests coincide with our interests are to do with the constituency we are serving, because obviously we cover stuff that is outside of the constituencies of those two arts councils. So the Arts Council of Northern Ireland is concerned with supporting arts in Northern Ireland. Other than that their concerns are to do with things like keeping accurate finances and things like that. They don't have an idea of what a photography magazine should be...

Right up until 2001 when I left 'Creative Camera' photography was highly politicized in the Arts Council. I am asking, rhetorically I suppose, if a photography magazine can exist outside of the pressures of the "business"?

Maybe it is impossible to do it in London. It does come back round to the fact that we are in Belfast. It manifests itself in every aspect of the magazine. We are as interested in what happens in the Northern Gallery of Contemporary Art, that do a lot of photography exhibitions, as we are in the Photographers' Gallery. We are as interested in what happens in Warsaw or in Edinburgh. The institutions in London are obviously quite powerful, there are great collections there.. As far as we can see being in Belfast gives you a great perspective to give all these institutions across the country parity.

Does all this say something about Northern Ireland or something about these times. That the politics around photography have simply slipped away. It probably says a lot about the Arts Council of England; of course we had dealings with ...

Do you think 'Source' advances an agenda for change?

Well, yes there is a sort of ethic to do with how work is treated and to do with respect due to people who are producing work.

That is more like your values. Is there also a catalyst function?

The catalyst function is probably to do with the things we find stimulating, so for instance the discussion we had about Sebald. It's not that we had a mission to generate this change but I think you see this stuff bubbling up and you think I want to find other books like this, review them and that this will provoke discussion.

Is this dare I say, a function of testing what is understood by "photography"?

Dare away. Sebald was not just the novelty, it goes back to something I was saying earlier on about the nature of photography, that it allows conversations about many different things.

For me photography became just too freighted. You seem to be talking about text-image relationships when you describe your favourite content. And that area of text-image is entirely unpoliticised by comparison. Even though you're in Belfast and nobody is pressurizing you, there is this history that – even if you do not acknowledge its influence – you and your contributors are alluding to, arguing with, ignoring it deliberately and so on. You have no control over that.

I can see that this photographic history – that is 30 years of people arguing about photography. It is debilitating because it is fractious and it is easy to get bogged down in it. But I think if you can escape all that drag...

I am saying that you can't escape.

It doesn't have to be a drag.

No, but what I am saying is that much is prescribed. The book Art? Was sort of a metaphor for a process that was happening all round the world (the rejection of Greenbergian aesthetics and post modernism). Exactly the same thing happened at 'Creative Camera' in 1980 when everybody divided into modernists and postmodernists. That was symbolic of a change that happened not just in London but all over the world. This says that there is a larger, inscribed history here to the world you work in. That is part of the context and you're right it doesn't have to be a drag but it's there.

Of course, yeah. It's probably invisible to a degree but we are in a bigger context. And the photography world is just a bit if that.

My desire at 'Creative Camera' had always been to step outside of the photography context and find something (maybe like text and image) which was fresh and offered a chance to use new perspectives.

You make it sound as if you never wanted to do a photography magazine.

I did. But I knew immediately how difficult it would be to do something I wanted. Everyone I have interviewed seems to have had one thing they wanted to do with their magazine. There was always an agenda. And when magazines are at their best they make things happen. Is there a mission?

(You answered it but I never recorded the answer)

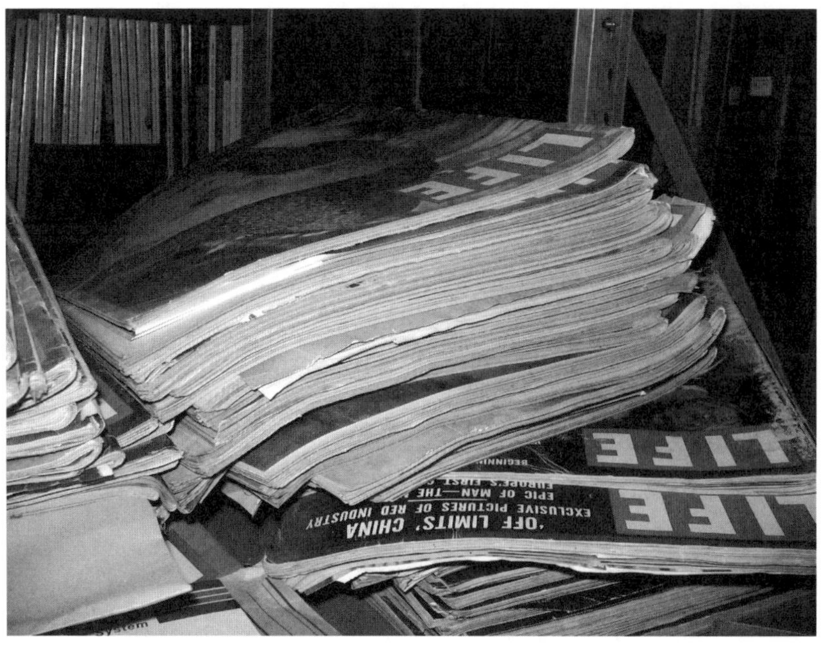
LIFE
'OFF LIMITS' CHINA
EXCLUSIVE PICTURES OF RED INDUSTRY
EPIC OF MAN—THE
LIFE

About the Authors

David Brittain has been active in photography as a curator, critic, lecturer and as editor of the respected international magazine 'Creative Camera' (1991-2001). He has contributed to a wide range of publications and has been involved in the production of various documentaries for BBC TV programmes such as 'The Late Show' and the 'Decisive Moments' series. In 2000 his anthology of writings, 'Creative Camera: 30 Years of Writing' was published by Manchester University Press.

In 2002 David was awarded an AHRC Fellowship in the Creative and Performing Arts to research the subject of photography and the self-published magazine.

Clinton Cahill is an artist, designer and educator based at the Manchester School of Art. His creative practice encompasses painting, graphic design and illustration, with a particular research interest in the relationships between text, illustration and the phenomenology of the image which is focused on a long-term study of visuality of James Joyce's 'Finnegans Wake'. Clinton's illustrated blog 'Illuminating the Wake' has become a regular feature on the website of the James Joyce Centre, Dublin.

Bibliography and resources

Batchen, G. (1999). After Postmodernism. In J. Annear, E. McDonald (eds.) *What is this thing called photography?: Australian Photography 1975-1985,* New South Wales: Pluto Press/Art Gallery of New South Wales, pp. 74-81.

Brereton, K. (1990). Photo-Discourse: Critical theory and practice in Australia, in J. Annear, E. McDonald (eds.) *What is this thing called photography?: Australian Photography 1975-1985*, New South Wales: Pluto Press/Art Gallery of New South Wales. pp. 64-73.

Brittain, D. (2000). *Creative Camera: 30 Years of Writing*, Manchester: Manchester University Press.

Brittain, D. (2005). Persistence of Vision: Current Photography Magazines in Britain, in *to be continued ... Helsinki: catalogue of the Helsinki Photography festival.*

Brittain, D. (2007). The Photographers' Press in the USA and Britain During the Transition Decade of the 60s, in F. Frey, T. Lopez, D. Malin, M. Osterman, M. Peres, G. Romer, N. Stuart, S. Williams. (eds.) *Focal Press Encyclopedia of Photography (fourth edition)*, London: Focal Press.

Bunell, P. (2012). *Aperture Magazine Anthology: The Minor White Years, 1952-1976*, New York: Aperture.

Coleman A.D. (2001). Toward Critical Mass: Writing and Publishing about Photography in the Boston Area, 1955-1985, in R. Lafo, G. Nagler (eds.), *Photography in Boston: 1955-1985,* Massachusetts: DeCordova Museum and Sculpture Park and MIT Press.

Ilzawa, K. (2003). Major Photography Magazines, in A. Tucker (ed.) *The History of Japanese Photography,* Hudston: Huston Museum of Fine Arts.

Kelly O. and Landry C. (1986). Distribution and publication, in Bezencenet S. and Corigan P. (eds.) *Photographic Practices: Towards a Different Image,* Comedia.

Myers K. (1986). Camerawork, in Bezencenet S. and Corigan P. (eds.) *Photographic Practices: Towards a Different Image*, Comedia.

North, M.(2005). 'Camera Works: Photography and the Twentieth-Century Word', Oxford, Oxford University Press.

Taylor, J. (1986). 'Photographic Practices: Towards a Different Image' in S. Bezencenet and P. Corigan (eds.) *Photographic Practices: Towards a Different Image.* London: Comedia.

Periodicals

Brittain, D. (1997). Creative Camera, *Photofile*, April 1997, pp. 38-41.

Brittain, D. (2010). Found, Shared The Magazine Photowork, *Visual Communication* Volume 8, (No 4).

Bull, S. (1999). 'The Return of Theory (in colour): Photography Magazines in the 1990s,' *Source photographic review,* Issue 21, Winter.

Coleman, A.D. (1999). The Heart of the Literature: 'Little Magazines of photography in the U.S.', *Source photographic review*, Issue 21, Winter.

Fondiller, H.(1981). Tome Maloney and US Camera, *Camera Arts*, July/August 1981.

Jolly, M. (1997). A Brief History of Photofile, *Photofile,* April 1997, pp. 33-37.

Green, J. (1979). Aperture in the 50s: the word and the way, *Afterimage,* March 1979.

Kaufhold, E. (1999). From the North, *Source photographic review,* Issue 21, Winter.

Koetzle, H. (2009). Art and Publishing European Photography's Anniversary, *European Photography,* No 85/86.

Millar, A.J. (2004). The Alchemy of Layout, *Eye* magazine, Issue 51.

Misani, M. (1978). Survey of photography magazines, *Printletter, No* 13.

Monk, L. (1979). Excerpts from A Talk by Lorraine Monk, *Photocommuniqué*, Vol 1 March/ April.

Osman, C. (1988). The Printed Photo at Photokina, *Creative Camera*, October.

Esparza, R. (1999). The Difficulty of Diffusion, *Source photographic review*, Issue 21, Winter.

Schmid, J. (1999). Dispose of this Magazine Carefully After Use, *Source photographic review,* issue 21, Winter.

Toshiya U. (2003). Rethinking The Cultural and Spatial Turn in Japanese Photography: A Psycho-Photo-Geography of Japan, *Camera Austria*, Issue 84.

Tucker A. (1981). The Photo League, *Ovo,* Issue 40/41.

Various authors, (2004/5). Forum: Creative Camera, *Photoworks*, Autumn/Winter.

Anon (1993). 'The Provoke Era', *Déjà Vu* No 14.

Web sites

Brittain, D. (2002) One for the Money, Two for the Show, http://fine-photographs.co.uk/index.php/creative-camera-all/one-for-the-money (Accessed 09 06 2013).

Brittain, D. (2002) Peter Turner Obituary, http://fine-photographs.co.uk/index.php/creative-camera-editors/peter-turner-by-david-brittain (Accessed 09 06 2013).

For information about Ten.8:
Birmingham City Archives (2005) Derek Bishton and Ten.8, http://www.connectinghistories.org.uk/collections/bishton.asp, (Accessed 09 08 2013).

Jay, B. (2004) Magazine Memoirs: Creative Camera and Album 1968-1972, http://www.billjayonphotography.com/Magazine%20Memoirs.pdf (Accessed 09 08 2103).

Past issues of Reportage:
Reportage web site (2001), http://www.reportage.org, (Accessed 09 08 2013).

The Impulse archive of back issues:
Impulse web site (2008) http://www.eldongarnet.com/impulse_71.71.asp, (Accessed 09 08 2013).

Information about Source Photographic Review:
Source Photographic Review, http://www.source.ie/index.php (Accessed 09 08 2013).

Information about Photofile:
http://www.acp.org.au/photofile (Accessed 09 08 2013).

Oral history

British Library, Oral History of British Photography contains relevant interviews with Bill Jay, Colin Osman and Peter Turner.

Exhibitions containing photographers' magazines

'Artist's Magazines', 'Visual Studies Workshop', Nov 26 1980-January 9 1981.

'Dream Street: W. Eugene Smith's Pittsburgh Photographs', March 27-June 16 2002 ICP, New York.

'Found, Shared: the Magazine Photowork', curated by David Brittain for CUBE gallery, Manchester, Spring 2006 and the Photographers' Gallery, London, Summer 2007.